TOURISTS' BEHAVIORS AND EVALUATIONS

ADVANCES IN CULTURE, TOURISM AND HOSPITALITY RESEARCH

Series Editor: Arch G. Woodside

Recent Volumes:

ADVANCES IN CULTURE, TOURISM AND HOSPITALITY
RESEARCH   VOLUME 9

TOURISTS' BEHAVIORS AND EVALUATIONS

EDITED BY

ARCH G. WOODSIDE
Boston College, Chestnut Hill, MA, USA

METIN KOZAK
Dokuz Eylul University, İzmir, Turkey

United Kingdom − North America − Japan
India − Malaysia − China

Emerald Group Publishing Limited
Howard House, Wagon Lane, Bingley BD16 1WA, UK

First edition 2014

British Library Cataloguing in Publication Data
A catalogue record for this book is available from the British Library

ISBN: 978-1-78441-172-5
ISSN: 1871-3173 (Series)

Printed and bound by CPI Group (UK) Ltd, Croydon, CR0 4YY

ISOQAR certified
Management System,
awarded to Emerald
for adherence to
Environmental
standard
ISO 14001:2004.

Certificate Number 1985
ISO 14001

INVESTOR IN PEOPLE

CONTENTS

LIST OF CONTRIBUTORS

Suzan Becks	Open University, Heerlen, The Netherlands
P. Monica Chien	University of Queensland, Brisbane, Australia
Chien-Fen Chiu	Arizona State University, Phoenix, AZ, USA
Andy S. Choi	University of Queensland, Brisbane, Australia
Hwansuk Chris Choi	University of Guelph, Guelph, Canada
Antónia Correia	CEFAGE, Universidade do Algarve, Faro, Portugal
Yesim Cosar	Dokuz Eylul University, İzmir, Turkey
Alain Decrop	University of Namur, Namur, Belgium
Yosuke Endo	Tokyo Metropolitan University, Tokyo, Japan
Andrew J. Frew	Queen Margaret University, Edinburgh, UK
Tamara Jovanovic	University of Novi Sad, Novi Sad, Serbia
Metin Kozak	Dokuz Eylul University, İzmir, Turkey
Yohei Kurata	Tokyo Metropolitan University, Tokyo, Japan
Lidija Lalicic	Modul University, Vienna, Austria
Woojin Lee	Arizona State University, Phoenix, AZ, USA
Xiang (Robert) Li	University of South Carolina, Columbia, SC, USA

Julie Masset	University of Namur, Namur, Belgium
Karlan Muniz	Pontifícia Universidade Católica, do Paraná, Paraná, Brazil
Taketo Naoi	Tokyo Metropolitan University, Tokyo, Japan
Brent W. Ritchie	University of Queensland, Brisbane, Australia
Paulo M. M. Rodrigues	Banco de Portugal, Universidade Nova de Lisboa, Lisboa, Portugal
Mareba M. Scott	Queen Margaret University, Edinburgh, UK
Jaime Serra	CEFAGE, Universidade de Évora, Évora, Portugal
HeeKyung Sung	Arizona State University, Phoenix, AZ, USA
Bernadette M. Watson	University of Queensland, Brisbane, Australia
Arch G. Woodside	Boston College, Chestnut Hill, MA, USA

PREFACE

Readers of Volume 9 of the ACTHR series will find the following 11 chapters to be, not only of use to their obtaining an understanding of the development of new research skills, but a delightful read as well. All chapters focus directly or indirectly on tourists' behaviors and evaluations. The chapters appear in alphabetical order according to the first author's family name. Here is a brief introduction to each chapter.

CARBON OFFSETTING BEHAVIOR

In the first chapter, "Air Travelers' Carbon Offsetting Behavior: An Experimental Study," Andy S. Choi and Brent W. Ritchie investigate how general and behavior specific attitudes work together in explaining air travelers' carbon offsetting behavior.

EVALUATING SERVICE PERFORMANCE

In the second chapter, "Evaluation of the Service Performance: Application of the Zone of Tolerance with Importance Performance Analysis of a Convention Facility," Hwansuk Chris Choi, Woojin Lee, HeeKyung Sung, and Chien-Fen Chiu compare the applicability of the zone of tolerance and importance-performance analysis (IPA) techniques in the evaluation of convention delegates' perceptions of products and services.

SLOW TOURISM

In the third chapter, "Slow Tourism (Cittaslow) Influence over Visitors' Behavior," Yesim Cosar and Metin Kozak investigate the extent to which the image of a slow city motivates domestic tourists to visit a destination. Also, the authors investigate the impact of the slow city on visitors' behavior, in terms of information search, decision making, holiday experience, and post-holiday experience.

TOURISTS' SOUVENIRS

In the fourth chapter, "A T-shirt from New York, a Coral from Mauritius: A Functional Typology of Tourist Souvenirs," Alain Decrop and Julie Masset offer a deeper understanding of the symbols and meanings attached to tourists' special possessions as well as of the functions they fulfill in contemporary consumption.

EXHIBITION AREAS

In the fifth paper, "Exhibition Areas: Case Study Research of Japanese Firms," Yosuke Endo, Yohei Kurata, and Taketo Naoi describe the potential of exhibition areas operated by consumer goods companies as a method of relationship marketing for corporate branding.

INDIVIDUAL VALUES AND HOLIDAY PREFERENCES

In the sixth chapter, "Individual Values and Holiday Preferences," Tamara Jovanovic explores the relationship between individual values and holiday preference. She shows that values can be standards of assessing behaviors in tourism research and values connect tourists' behaviors and activities preferences.

PARENTHOOD AND HOLIDAY DECISIONS: A GROUNDED THEORY APPROACH

In the seventh chapter, "Parenthood and Holiday Decisions: A Grounded Theory Approach," Lidija Lalicic and Suzan Becks investigate how holiday decisions for couples change when they become parents. The authors discuss 10 in-depth interviews with Dutch parents-to-be, expecting their first child. The results show that emotional response ranks high in terms of the occurred changes, which originate from a set of interrelated consequences.

TOURISTS' RISK PERCEPTIONS

In the eighth paper, "It Can't Happen to Me: Travel Risk Perceptions," Brent W. Ritchie, P. Monica Chien, and Bernadette M. Watson introduce new theory to explain how people calibrate travel risks; the conceptual model incorporates constructs from motivational theories, cognitive appraisal, and emotionality.

ADOPTING NEW TECHNOLOGIES WHILE TRAVELING

In the ninth chapter, "Adoption of Information and Communications Technology (ICT) by In-Trip Leisure Tourists," Mareba M. Scott and Andrew J. Frew examine factors influencing actual in-trip ICT usage by leisure tourists and the potential of adopted technologies to support sustainable tourism; a thematic analysis of the data revealed that consistent with the literature perceived ease of use, perceived usefulness and social influence affected usage while in-trip.

HETEROGENEITY IN TOURISM MOTIVATIONS HAPPENS

In the tenth chapter, "Heterogeneity in Tourism Motivations: The Case of the Algarve," Jaime Serra, CEFAGE, Antónia Correia, and Paulo M. M. Rodrigues use data from visitors to the Algarve (Portugal) to identify 10 main motivations and reveal that these are statistically different by origin countries and over the years.

CONFIGURAL ANALYSIS USING FUZZY SET QUALITATIVE COMPARATIVE ANALYSIS

In the eleventh chapter, "Configural Modeling of Country-Collectors Motives, Behavior, and Assessments of Strengths of National-Place Brands," Arch G. Woodside, Xiang (Robert) Li, and Karlan Muniz offer an early workbench model of antecedents, paths, and outcomes of country collectors' evaluations and behavior toward countries as place-brands competing for such visitors.

CONCLUSION

The chapters in this volume are more daring and provocative in developing new theory and/or in the methods to test tenets of specific theories than what is typically available in articles in scholarly journals. Similar to prior volumes in the ACTHR series, the following chapters apply different recipes that include useful new knowledge in easy-to-read formats. The promise is made and kept here for an enjoyable, insightful, and memorable learning experience. Enjoy!

A NOTE OF APPRECIATION AND AN INVITATION

The authors and editors of this volume are grateful for the encouragement by members of staff of Emerald Group Publishing Limited, especially Rebecca Evans and Daniel Berze, in seeing this volume to completion. The authors and editors express their gratitude to the in-depth (2,500 + words per review) comments by all members of the ACTHR Editorial Advisory Board (EAB). All chapters were improved via the blind reviews by members of the EAB.

The ACTHR Series Editor (Arch G. Woodside) asks all readers who are working in institutions with members of the EAB to take a moment to thank them personally — work in serving as a member of an EAB is usually under-recognized while being extremely valuable in improving the quality of manuscripts. Please review the listing of EAB members and their affiliations appearing in the front pages to select one to a few colleagues to thank. Thank you for doing so!

The authors and editors invite the reader to participate as an author in future volumes of the ACTHR series and to join the Academy of Culture, Tourism and Hospitality Research. Information about the Academy and the steps to become a member are available at http://www.iacthlr.com/.

Arch G. Woodside
Metin Kozak
Editors

EDITORIAL BOARD

AIR TRAVELERS' CARBON OFFSETTING BEHAVIOR: AN EXPERIMENTAL STUDY

Andy S. Choi and Brent W. Ritchie

ABSTRACT

Following the hierarchical model of human behavior of Fulton, Manfredo, and Lipscomb (1996), this chapter develops and tests a model incorporating both general and behavior-specific components of motivation. The research aimed to investigate how general and behavior-specific attitudes work together in explaining air travelers' carbon offsetting behavior. The study is an experimental study that applied confirmatory factor analysis using structural equation models to better understand the motivational factors that influence aviation carbon offsetting behavior. The sample includes 349 staff and students of the University of Queensland. Based on an established hierarchical model of human behavior, the new ecological paradigm (NEP) scale and the theory of planned behavior work together to explicate general and specific attitudes, respectively. The effect from NEP to offsetting intention was partially mediated by three intermediate motivations: awareness of climate impacts of air traveling, perceived effectiveness of carbon offsets in mitigating carbon emissions, and support for a carbon tax. In particular,

Tourists' Behaviors and Evaluations
Advances in Culture, Tourism and Hospitality Research, Volume 9, 1–7
ISSN: 1871-3173/doi:10.1108/S1871-317320140000009001

general support for the carbon price policy showed a complementary relationship with voluntary action.

Keywords: Carbon offsets; motivation; new ecological paradigm; theory of planned behavior; air travel

INTRODUCTION

According to Gössling, Haglund, Kallgren, Revahl, and Hultman (2009), air travel is one of the most intensive human activities in terms of carbon emissions. Air travel is also responsible for about half of the overall tourism carbon footprint, and this proportion continues to increase (UNWTO/ UNEP/WMO, 2008). Australia's major airlines have operated "fly carbon neural" programs that provide opportunities for air travelers to purchase voluntary carbon offsets since 2007. The Australian government also introduced a mandatory payment mechanism with a carbon price of $23 per ton of CO_2 in July 2012. Subsequently, one may expect to see the crowding-out effect of Bowles (2008), arguing that the carbon price policy attenuates voluntary action.

The literature of aviation carbon offsets is silent about this relationship between the newly implemented carbon price and voluntary carbon offset behavior, while motivational factors for voluntary behavior received much attention (Brouwer, Brander, & Van Beukering, 2008; Gössling et al., 2009; Lu & Shon, 2012; Mair, 2011). However, the relationships among these factors have not been clearly identified and not much is known about how they interact together in explaining air travelers' carbon offsetting behavior. Addressing this knowledge gap, this chapter aims to develop a behavioral model that incorporates major motivational factors to assess their influence on the carbon offsetting behavior.

Voluntary carbon offset programs of airline companies offer a unique research scope for researchers to gain insights into salient motivational factors for this type of voluntary behaviors. This is particularly true and timely as global carbon markets (including the EU emission trading program) experience a record low price for carbon. The literature provides various potential motivational factors, empirically or conceptually, while ignores their relationships. This study is the first to our knowledge to incorporate these factors and to suggest a behavioral model, particularly before a carbon tax is formally introduced. The findings not only demonstrate a complementary relationship between voluntary payments and a carbon tax but also identify the key areas for policy interventions.

THEORETICAL CONSIDERATIONS

Human behaviors can be explained at multiple, hierarchical levels (Ajzen, 1991; Eagly & Chaiken, 1993; Fulton, Manfredo, & Lipscomb, 1996; Stern, 2000). According to the behavioral model of Fulton et al. (1996), for example, fundamental values and value orientations are the most abstract forms of motivations that drive more specific attitudes and behavioral intention. These attitudinal constructs are normally generalized as general attitudes and behavior-specific attitudes. This generalization is in line with other well established behavioral models such as the attitude-behavior model of Eagly and Chaiken (1993), the value-belief-norm theory of Stern (2000), and theory of planned behavior (TPB) of Ajzen (1991). General attitudes take more time to change, thus more stable, than behavior-specific attitudes and are often indirectly related to specific behaviors.

The generalized behavioral model can easily incorporate major motivational factors. The literature offers a list of motivational factors, such as support for a price mechanism (CARP) (Brouwer et al., 2008), awareness of flight-caused carbon emissions (FLYCAR) (Brouwer et al., 2008; Gössling et al., 2009), and perceived effectiveness of the voluntary offset programs in addressing climate change (EFFECT) (Lu & Shon, 2012). According to Ajzen (1991), attitudes toward objects (i.e., a carbon price) influence evaluation of cognitive beliefs, and then specific behaviors. Thus, this study classified these factors as intermediate attitudes.

METHOD

An online survey was used with questionnaires that were developed through two focus groups and a pre-test. Questionnaires included various questions about individual attitudes and cognitive beliefs. In order to measure general environmental attitudes, this study adapted the new ecological paradigm (NEP) scale of Dunlap, Van Liere, Mertig, and Jones (2000) so that a shorter version with 10 statements[1] was employed. The TPB (Ajzen, 1991) was employed to measure behavior-specific attitudes. The underlying idea of this measurement scale is that attitudes toward the behavior (ATT), subjective norms (SN), and perceived behavioral control (PBC) influence people's behavioral intention (INT). As to the intermediate motivations, three statements were devised and evaluated on a seven-point scale: "Do you agree that your flights contribute to climate change?" for FLYCAR; "My paying for voluntary carbon offsets will reduce carbon emissions" for EFFECT; and "Do you support a carbon price under the Clean Energy Future Plan?" for CARP.

Participants in the survey were students and staff members of the University of Queensland. Online survey was carried out for a week in late June 2012, right before the implementation of the mandatory carbon price. A total of 346 useful responses were collected. Among the participants, 50% were students and 69% were female. In order to address the issue of skewed distributions, the Bollen–Stine bootstrapping method was employed with 2,000 bootstraps (Bollen & Stine, 1992).

FINDINGS

Fig. 1 shows that the developed behavioral model that has a good fit $(\chi^2 = 5.99,\ df = 3,$ Bollen–Steine bootstrap $p = 0.1079,\ \chi^2/df = 1.9963,$

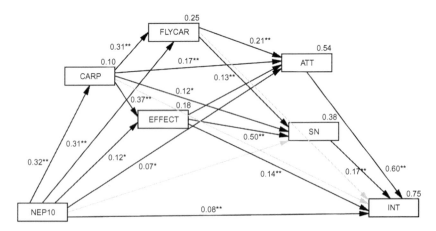

Fig. 1. The Final Structural Equation Model. *Notes*: NEP, new ecological paradigm; CARP, support for a carbon price; FLYCAR, awareness of flight-caused climate change; EFFECT, perceived effectiveness of voluntary carbon offsets; ATT, attitudes; SN, subjective norms; INT, offsetting intention. $*p < 0.05, **p < 0.01.$

RMSEA = 0.0537, CFI = 0.9975, SRMR = 0.0160) (Hu & Bentler, 1999). Four different types of attitudinal measures in the conceptual models and multiple variables for intermediate and specific attitudes provided 19 individual paths. Among these paths, three regression weights were not significant at the 0.05 level; between NEP and SN, between CARP and INT, and between FLYCAR and INT. In particular, the positively significant effect from CARP to ATT and SN indicates a complementary relationship between the mandatory and voluntary payments.

CONCLUSION AND IMPLICATIONS

This study developed a behavioral model for voluntary carbon offsets. This model was able to explain how major motivational factors interact with other attitudinal measures at different levels in determining people's offsetting intention, particularly prior to the introduction of a new carbon price. General environmental attitudes showed both direct and indirect effects on INT, partially mediated by intermediate and specific attitudes. All intermediate motivations not only showed a positive and significant effect on the specific attitudes (ATT and SN), but also their effects on INT were mostly fully mediated by the latter, except for EFFECT. The direct path between EFFECT and INT remained significant, showing a partial mediation by ATT and SN. In particular, the three intermediate attitudes (CARP, FLYCAR, and EFFECT) showed a partial mediation for the path between NEP and ATT, and a full mediation between NEP and SN. Based on these findings, if policy intervention was necessary to bring changes in travelers' offsetting behavior, the target areas might be the intermediate attitudes, mainly due to the feasibility of changing attitudes and influencing behavioral intentions.

This study has some limitations. Three intermediate variables were only considered and measured with single items. Further, the sample was limited to university students and staff. Although nonrepresentative samples such as student samples are not rare in examining latent constructs (MacKerron, Egerton, Gaskell, Parpia, & Mourato, 2009), however, unexpected differences might exist for more representative samples. It should be also noted that future changes in the behavioral model need to be examined further under the carbon price policy.

NOTE

1. This study included items 1, 3, 5, 6, 7, 8, 9, 12, 14, and 15. Two items represent each of the five "theorised" facets of the NEP scale (Dunlap et al., 2000).

ACKNOWLEDGMENT

We acknowledge that some contents in this chapter are reprinted from our journal article with a similar title.

REFERENCES

Ajzen, I. (1991). The theory of planned behavior. *Organizational Behavior and Human Decision Processes, 50*, 179−211.

Bollen, K. A., & Stine, R. A. (1992). Bootstrapping goodness-of-fit measures in structural equation models. *Sociological Methods & Research, 21*(2), 205−229.

Bowles, S. (2008). Policies designed for self-interested citizens may undermine "the moral sentiments": Evidence from economic experiments. *Science, 320*(5883), 1605−1609.

Brouwer, R., Brander, L., & Van Beukering, P. (2008). A convenient truth: Air travel passengers' willingness to pay to offset their CO_2 emissions. *Climatic Change, 90*(3), 299−313.

Dunlap, R. E., Van Liere, K. D., Mertig, A. G., & Jones, R. E. (2000). Measuring endorsement of the new ecological paradigm: A revised NEP scale. *Journal of Social Issues, 56*(3), 425−442.

Eagly, A. H., & Chaiken, S. (1993). *Psychology of attitudes*. Fort Worth, TX: Harcourt Brace Jovanovich.

Fulton, D. C., Manfredo, M. J., & Lipscomb, J. (1996). Wildlife value orientations: A conceptual and measurement approach. *Human Dimensions of Wildlife, 1*(2), 24−47.

Gössling, S., Haglund, L., Kallgren, H., Revahl, M., & Hultman, J. (2009). Swedish air travelers and voluntary carbon offsets: Towards the co-creation of environmental value? *Current Issues in Tourism, 12*(1), 1−19.

Hu, L., & Bentler, P. M. (1999). Cutoff criteria for fit indexes in covariance structure analysis: Conventional criteria versus new alternatives. *Structural Equation Modeling: A Multidisciplinary Journal, 6*(1), 1−55.

Lu, J.-L., & Shon, Z. Y. (2012). Exploring airline passengers' willingness to pay for carbon offsets. *Transportation Research Part D − Transport and Environment, 17*(2), 124−128.

MacKerron, G. J., Egerton, C., Gaskell, C., Parpia, A., & Mourato, S. (2009). Willingness to pay for carbon offset certification and co-benefits among (high-)flying young adults in the UK. *Energy Policy, 37*(4), 1372−1381.

Mair, J. (2011). Exploring air travelers' voluntary carbon-offsetting behavior. *Journal of Sustainable Tourism, 19*(2), 215−230.

Stern, P. C. (2000). Toward a coherent theory of environmentally significant behavior. *Journal of Social Issues, 56*(3), 407–424.

UNWTO/UNEP/WMO. (2008). *Climate change and tourism: Responding to global challenges.* Madrid, Spain: World Tourism Organization and United Nations Environment Programme. Retrieved from http://www.unep.fr/shared/publications/pdf/WEBx0142xPA-ClimateChangeandTourismGlobalChallenges.pdf

EVALUATION OF THE SERVICE PERFORMANCE: APPLICATION OF THE ZONE OF TOLERANCE WITH IMPORTANCE PERFORMANCE ANALYSIS OF A CONVENTION FACILITY

Hwansuk Chris Choi, Woojin Lee, HeeKyung Sung and Chien-Fen Chiu

ABSTRACT

This study compares the applicability of the zone of tolerance (ZOT) and importance performance analysis (IPA) techniques in the evaluation of convention delegates' perceptions of products and services. Overall, 217 out of 400 were used for analysis, providing a response rate of 54%. The study results indicated that although an IPA technique is still useful in assessing the service performance of a convention facility, IPA should be employed with caution, concrete criteria, and clear goals. The study

Tourists' Behaviors and Evaluations
Advances in Culture, Tourism and Hospitality Research, Volume 9, 9–19
ISSN: 1871-3173/doi:10.1108/S1871-317320140000009000

results also showed that the ZOT is practically applicable into business practice to assess service performance item by item.

Keywords: Zone of tolerance; importance performance analysis; three-factor theory; service quality; convention center

INTRODUCTION

In the past, convention research heavily focused on the economic impact of the convention industry and the decision-making process concerning the convention site (Crouch & Richie, 1998). Given the growing competiveness of the convention industry, a thorough understanding of service performance has become more important than ever. Along with this trend, recent convention studies examine attendees' needs, service performance (quality) factors, service priorities, and motivations (Severt, Wang, Chen, & Breiter, 2007). In such, it has become critical for organizations to build their strategies with attention given to key factors in service performance.

To develop and implement a strategic approach, organizations need to understand how their customers perceive the key elements of service performance. Several models and methods have been used in marketing research. One proven method is important performance analysis (IPA). The IPA provides strategically useful information to take corrective action, and build and maintain competitive advantages. Another technique used to assess service performance is zone of tolerance (ZOT), which is a range of customers' expectations of service (Zeithaml, Berry, & Parasuraman, 1993). This chapter examines convention delegates' perceptions of product and service performance of a convention facility by applying IPA and ZOT.

THEORETICAL CONSIDERATIONS

Importance Performance Analysis

As the convention industry becomes increasingly competitive, delivering quality service is essential (e.g., Randall & Senior, 1994). Therefore, the level of service quality affects an organization's competitiveness and performance and has been an important topic for research. One increasingly popular method used to assess the quality of service is the importance performance analysis (IPA), which examines customers' acceptance of product and service attributes (Martilla & James, 1977). Formulated by Martilla and James (1977), IPA views satisfaction in terms of the importance of service attributes to customers, as well as the performance of a service provider. These combined satisfaction ratings are plotted on a two-dimensional action grid, where the level of importance on the vertical axes and the level of performance on the horizontal axes of service attributes are compared (Joppe, Martin, & Waalen, 2001).

The Zone of Tolerance

The ZOT is a range of customers' expectations of service (Zeithaml et al., 1993). The ZOT provides information not only about customers' perceptions of service quality but also about the discrepancy between the desired services and those that are actually provided. Parasuraman, Berry, and Zeithaml (1991) applied SERVQUAL when assessing service performance by utilizing ZOT. Traditionally, researchers focused on the desired expectation as the only comparison standard to measure the gap between expectation and service quality (Walker & Baker, 2000). To understand customers' service expectations, Parasuraman et al. (1991) proposed two levels of service expectation: desired and adequate service. Desired expectation is the level of service that customers wish to receive; adequate service is the minimum level of service that customers are willing to accept (Parasuraman et al., 1991). Adequate service is not as good as desired service, and the separation between the two is the ZOT (Parasuraman, 2004). Hence, if customers' perceived level of service falls within the zone, they are still satisfied with service delivered (i.e., competitive advantage). If the service is better than the level of desired service, customers consider the service to be outstanding (i.e., customer franchise). However, if the service is less than adequate, customers are dissatisfied (i.e., competitive disadvantage) (Parasuraman et al., 1991; Parasuraman, 2004).

Three-Factor Theory

Many studies have reported that the five dimensions of service quality are not stable (e.g., Campos & Nobrega, 2009). In such, some researchers have suggested that service performance can be better measured with two or three dimensions. Matzler and Sauerwein (2002) suggest a comprehensive, three-factor structure of customer satisfaction based on previous research on customer satisfaction: basic, performance, and excitement. Basic factors are minimum requirements that cause dissatisfaction if not fulfilled, but do not lead to customer satisfaction if fulfilled or exceeded (p. 318). It is not a sufficient condition for satisfaction; rather, it is a threshold in order to enter the market (Füller & Matzler, 2008).

At the same time, performance factors are directly linked to customers' needs and desires; consequently, performance factors lead to satisfaction if fulfilled or exceeded and lead to dissatisfaction if not. Excitement factors increase customer satisfaction if services are delivered, but do not cause dissatisfaction if they are missing (Füller & Matzler, 2008; Matzler & Sauerwein, 2002). Since these services are provided to customers beyond their needs and expectations, there is nothing to decrease their satisfaction. With these points in mind, this study adopts Füller and Matzler's three-factor structure of service quality.

METHOD

Service quality items for a convention facility were extracted from the review of literature. Based on the consultation and pretest, 25 out of 38 services were selected for a survey questionnaire to test attendees' perceived level of importance and their perception of service performance. The study data was collected at the Phoenix Convention Center (PCC) and the population of this study was the International City/County Management Association's (ICMA) annual meeting attendees. Overall, 217 out of 400 attendees were used for analysis, providing a response rate of 54%.

FINDINGS

IPA Results

The importance/performance matrix is represented in Fig. 1(a)–(e). The average scores, neutral values, and grand means of each factor – basic, performance, and excitement – of the raw and actual performance were used as references in the IPA matrix. Based on the conservative IPA results shown in Fig. 1(a), 11 basic factor attributes fell into Quadrant II, except parking service (importance = 3.97 and performance = 4.70). Among seven performance service attributes, local food facilities and accommodation also fell into Quadrant II ("keep up the good work"). Four performance service attributes (in-house food service, business service, accommodation and food quality) were considered as low-priority areas of service provision. General food outlet is the only attribute that needs to be improved, including all the attributes in the other two factors. All of the excited factor attributes fall into either the low priority ("nightlife, cultural atmosphere, special food and tourist information") and possible overkill ("green efforts and light trail") quadrant.

Fig. 1(b) demonstrates the neutral point data (4 on a 7-point, Likert-type scale) plotting the importance and performance scores with horizontal

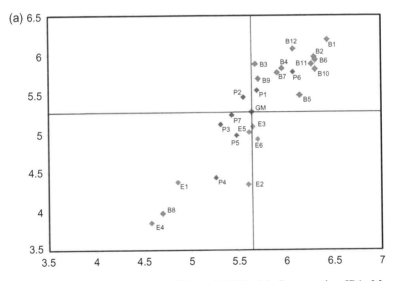

Fig. 1. Results of Data Analysis: IPA and ZOT. (a) Conservative IPA Matrix. (b) Liberal IPA Matrix. (c) IPA Matrix by Basic Factor. (d) IPA Matrix by Performance Factor. (e) IPA Matrix by Excitement Factor. (f) ZOT Analysis Result. *Notes: Basic Factor* – B1: Cleanliness, B2: Maintenance, B3: Comfort Seat, B4: Ventilation, B5: Public Space, B6: Restroom Access, B7: Wi-Fi Availability, B8: Parking Service, B9: Signage, B10: Friendly Staff, B11: Helpful Staff, B12: Safety. *Performance Factor* – P1: Local Food Facilities, P2: General Food Outlet, P3: In-house Food, P4: Business Service, P5: Road Signage, P6: Accommodation, P7: Food Quality. *Excitement Factor* – E1: Nightlife, E2: Cultural Atmosphere, E3: Green Effort, E4: Special Food, E5: Tourist Information, E6: Light Trail.

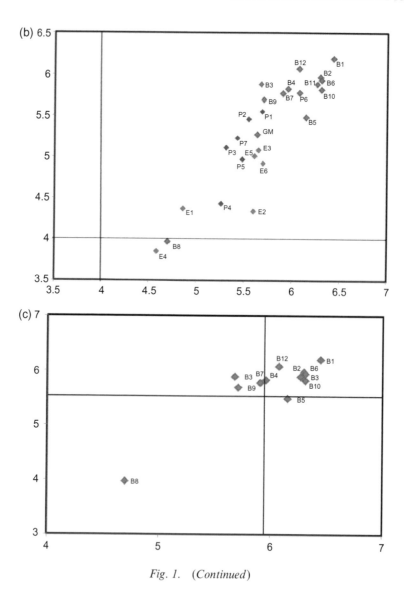

Fig. 1. (Continued)

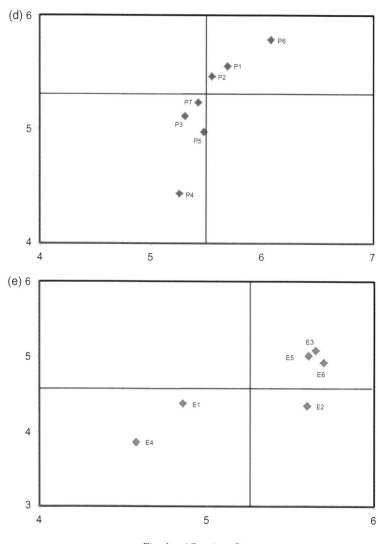

Fig. 1. (*Continued*)

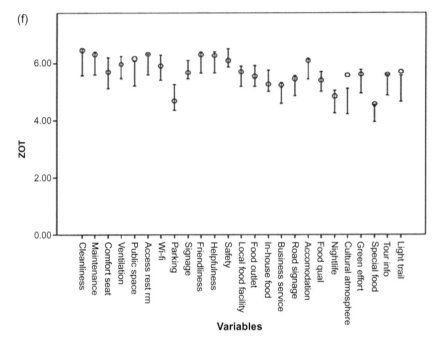

Fig. 1. (Continued)

and vertical gridlines, and the results are quite different from the conservative (traditional) IPA results earlier. All but two service quality attributes
are located in Quadrant II ("high satisfaction, high importance"); the
exceptions are parking service in the basic factor and special food in the
excitement factor, falling into Quadrant IV ("possible overkill").

Figs. 1(c)–(e) are importance-performance matrixes showing the overall
ratings of convention delegates' perceptions of PCC, using each factor's
grand means. The basic factor IPA grid shows some critical differences
from the results of conservative IPA. Service attributes, including
comfortable seating, Wi-Fi availability, and signage fell under the heading
of "concentrate efforts" here, while public space has achieved a high level
of performance, but it has been over-invested ("possible overkill").
Furthermore, the performance factor IPA results also provide the different
results from the conservative IPA results. Three service quality attributes
(local food facilities, general food outlet, and accommodation) fell into the
"keep up the good work" quadrant. From the results of the conservative

(traditional) IPA, no service attributes of the excitement factors were displayed in Quadrant II ("high importance, high performance") when applying the grand means as a cross-hair point. However, by utilizing the grand means of the excitement factor attributes (liberal IPA), "green efforts," "tourist information," and "light trail" fell into the "keep up the good work" quadrant, which provides the conflict results from the conservative IPA results.

ZOT Analysis Results

Fig. 1(f) presents the ZOT for the 25 service attributes in the box plot while the top and the bottom of the boxes are the means of respondents' desired and minimum level of expectations; additionally, the middle band represents the means of respondents' perceived service performance. Most of the respondents' perceived service performance was located within the ZOTs, which were close to the desired expectations at the top of the boxes, meaning that the respondents were highly satisfied. Exceptions were "public space" in the basic factor, as well as "light trail" and "cultural atmosphere," which indicate that the PCC's performance was higher than the respondents' desired expectations, representing possible overkill. In addition, four service attributes were relatively close to the minimum level of the delegates' perceived performance when compared with the other services: "parking service," "signage," "safety," and "in-house food." In other words, some of the respondents were not satisfied with these four service attributes provided by PCC. In such, PCC's performance failed to meet the minimum expectation of a certain segment of the respondents. This ZOT analysis result is equivalent to the concentrated efforts in the IPA matrix.

CONCLUSION AND IMPLICATIONS

The key lesson learned from this study's results is that IPA should be employed with caution, concrete criteria, and clear goals. The study's findings show that the improper use of the IPA application (i.e., the use of different cross-hair points) may lead to possible misinterpretation of the IPA analysis results. In such, defining a cross-hair point indicating high importance and high performance is a management decision based on the management team's experience and strategic goals.

The conservative IPA results show that most excitement factors fall into the low-priority quadrant, while the excitement factor IPA results in three attributes within the high-importance and high-performance category. The results of performance factor attributes for the two different approaches show similar results. In addition, most attributes fall in the "keep up the good work" quadrant in the liberal IPA results when employing neutral values as cross-hair points. Thus, without setting clear criteria and goals, these conflicting results can easily influence misleading interpretation of the study results. The IPA user must interpret the results with caution and pre-defined criteria. Furthermore, for practical use, a factor-based approach may work better than a conservative (traditional) approach, especially when applying a three-factor theory, because, unlike the equanimously important nature of a five-dimension service quality, the basic structure of a three-factor theory is hierarchical in nature.

Utilizing the multiple-expectation standards, the ZOT-enabled technique allows researchers and practitioners to deepen our understanding of customers' service expectations and to explore customers' tolerance levels toward each single service. Despite the fact that basic services have a narrower tolerance zone, respondents actually have the narrowest tolerance zone toward the performance services (zone width $= 0.71$) and have quite similar tolerance zones toward basic (zone width $= 0.78$) and excitement services (zone width $= 0.80$). This result indicates that the study respondents are relatively insensitive to both basic service and excitement factors. It can be argued that performance factor attributes are considered as a critical factor in building competitive advantages for PCC. Overall, the ZOT analysis results indicate that PCC provided high-quality service to their customers. However, it would be a challenge for the marketing managers to interpret the service attributes rated higher than desired expectation, because there are two ways to read this result: possible overkill versus delighted performance. Thus marketing managers should interpret the results with caution and with consideration of the organization's resource allocation and strategic goals.

Both techniques mainly utilize the means (actual or scale) of the service quality attributes; however, researchers and practitioners need to assess the attributes' standard deviations before employing either technique to assess their performance and customer expectations. Standard deviation is a useful tool to assess the dispersion of the study data. In other words, if the study data intervals (i.e., $-s < x < +s$) of certain service quality attributes are relatively large, that indicates a significant variation in responses. In practical terms, the service quality attributes with large standard deviation imply a possible discrepancy between certain groups toward expectation and performance; for example, satisfied versus unsatisfied, first time versus repeat visitors, delegates versus exhibitors or type of event attended that is held in a convention center (i.e., consumer and trade show, convention and conference). For instance, excitement factor attributes have relatively large standard deviations of both importance (ranging from 1.29 to 2.00) and performance (ranging from 1.13 to 1.75). Then, a segment-based analysis should be applied for both techniques. In this sense, both techniques can be used as a tool for identifying potential areas to be improved and to be used as a way to build competitive advantages at the initial stage of the strategic goal assessment.

REFERENCES

Campos, D. F., & Nobrega, K. C. (2009). Importance and zone of tolerance of customer expectations of fast food services. *The Flagship Research Journal of International Conference of the Production and Operations Management Society*, 2(2), 56–71.

Crouch, G. I., & Ritchie, J. R. B. (1998). Convention site selection research: A review, conceptual model, and propositional framework. *Journal of Convention and Exhibition Management*, 1(1), 49–69.

Füller, J., & Matzler, K. (2008). Customer delight and market segmentation: An application of the three-factor theory of customer satisfaction on life style groups. *Tourism Management*, 29(1), 116.

Joppe, M., Martin, D. W., & Waalen, J. (2001). Toronto's image as a destination: A comparative importance-satisfaction analysis by origin of visitor. *Journal of Travel Research*, 39(1), 252–260.

Martilla, J., & James, J. (1977). Importance-performance analysis. *Journal of Marketing*, 41(1), 77–79.

Matzler, K., & Sauerwein, E. (2002). The factor structure of customer satisfaction: An empirical test of the importance grid and the penalty-reward-contrast analysis. *International Journal of Service Industry Management*, 13(4), 314–332.

Parasuraman, A., Berry, L. L., & Zeithaml, V. A. (1991). Understanding customer expectations of service. *Sloan Management Review*, 32(3), 39–48.

Parasuraman, A. A. (2004). Assessing and improving service performance for maximum impact: Insights from a two-decade-long research journey. *Performance Measurement and Metrics*, 5(2), 45–52.

Randall, L., & Senior, M. (1994). A model for achieving quality in hospital hotel services. *International Journal of Contemporary Hospitality Management*, 6(1–2), 68–74.

Severt, D., Wang, Y., Chen, P., & Breiter, D. (2007). Examining the motivation, perceived performance, and behavioral intentions of convention attendees: Evidence from a regional conference. *Tourism Management*, 28, 399–408.

Walker, J., & Baker, J. (2000). An exploratory study of a multi-expectation framework for services. *Journal of Services Marketing*, 14(5), 411–431.

Zeithaml, V. A., Berry, L. L., & Parasuraman, A. (1993). The nature and determinants of customer expectations of service. *Journal of the Academy of Marketing Science*, 21(1), 1–12.

SLOW TOURISM (CITTASLOW) INFLUENCE OVER VISITORS' BEHAVIOR

Yesim Cosar and Metin Kozak

ABSTRACT

The purpose of this study is twofold: (1) to investigate the extent to which the image of a slow city motivates domestic tourists to visit a destination and (2) to investigate the impact of the slow city on visitors' behavior, in terms of information search, decision making, holiday experience, and post-holiday experience. To accomplish these objectives, the study follows the rules of qualitative research methods, conducting interviews with 24 domestic visitors to Seferihisar, Turkey's first accredited slow city. Our findings confirm that the image of a slow city influences the first three stages of visitor behavior, namely motivations, information search, and decision making. The study also shows that visitors had both positive and negative experiences during their holidays and that the slow city had a positive influence over their future intentions.

Keywords: Slow city (Cittaslow); sustainable tourism; visitor behavior; destination marketing

Tourists' Behaviors and Evaluations
Advances in Culture, Tourism and Hospitality Research, Volume 9, 21–29
Copyright © 2014 by Emerald Group Publishing Limited
All rights of reproduction in any form reserved
ISSN: 1871-3173/doi:10.1108/S1871-317320140000009002

INTRODUCTION

The tourism industry has changed considerably in recent years. While macro scale destination marketing is taking over micro level marketing at the individual organizational level, there has been much discussion about sustainable consumption and its reflection on tourism, as a result of the rapid development of the industry on one hand and the impact of globalization on the other. While there has been a remarkable increase in the number of projects supported by both the public and private sectors, due to changes on the demand side there is an increasing need to develop alternative product sets. Several new products have emerged as a result, and one of these is the concept of the "slow city."

The impact of globalization has been substantial over the last 20 years and has been felt in economic, cultural, political, and social life all around the world, and in all life circles. As a result, critical reactions and new movements for change have emerged. One such movement is the slow city, which began in 1989 with the slow food movement. The concept of a slow city is closely linked to the tourism industry, and is particularly associated with sustainable tourism and visitor behavior. However, there are very few empirical studies in the currently available literature on the influence of the slow city on visitor behavior as an attraction or tourism product. Thus, the purpose of this study is twofold: (1) to investigate the extent to which the image of a slow city motivates domestic tourists to visit a destination and (2) to investigate the impact of the slow city on visitors' behavior, in terms of information search, decision making, holiday experience, and post-holiday experience.

THEORETICAL CONSIDERATIONS

The concept of slowness stems from the thought that quickness causes chaos in the world. However, in many places where the impact of quickness or globalization has yet to make an impact, slowness is seen as the normal flow of man's daily life. As daily life patterns change, leading to an increasingly dynamic and hectic lifestyle, we find that the replacement and dependency on technology which results from globalization are at their lowest levels in those areas which are traditionally slow, and where a quiet lifestyle might still prevail. With 166 members in 25 countries, slow city is a union of cities' project, inspired by the slow food movement, which aims to counter the standardization of cities' characteristics and lifestyle and the elimination of local aspects which result from globalization (Mayer & Knox, 2006). Slow city is a union of cities and towns which resist homogenous places created by globalization, and which want to take their place on the world stage while at the same time protecting their local identity and characteristics. Slow city means determining the unique and characteristic areas of a city and developing strategies to protect them. It also means enjoying city life at a speed such that residents and visitors can enjoy the city's characteristics, color, music, and history in harmony.

The concept of the slow city is highly influenced by the introduction of slow food (Radstrom, 2005). Although the aims of the two movements are distinct, they are complimentary in several relevant respects. Both movements emphasize the protection of local and traditional culture, and both envisage spending time in a relaxed, slow, and enjoyable manner (Knox, 2005). With less traffic and lower populations, slow cities challenge the project of the bustling "homogenized world" which results from globalization (Knox, 2005). In the literature, a typical model of consumer behavior comprises five stages; however, it is possible to give an analyzing in just three phases: before purchasing, the moment of purchasing, and after purchasing (Engel, Blackwell, & Miniard, 1995). The following section provides a short overview of each phase of the model, with regards to the relationship between visitor behavior and the slow city.

Need Recognition

Although many factors have influenced the rapid development of tourism, the majority have emerged in order to serve the aim of meeting the psychological needs of individuals. For instance, the introduction or discovery of new attractions may address individuals' expectations of the prestige involved in having different experience and the desire to see new places. In accordance with fundamental consumer psychology, in certain cases consumers may act differently to others, and seek new products sets and brands (Singh, 2012). This tendency encourages service providers to develop new product sets and to create new brands. This variation serves to stimulate psychological needs, such as trying what has not been tried, trying what others have not tried, or escaping from hectic metropolitan city life.

Search for Information

Research shows that after the first phase of becoming aware of their needs, visitors apply to different sources to get detailed information on product sets which may meet their needs best. These sources are termed internal and external (Foodness & Murray, 1999). There are four different external sources: the first are visitor information offices and unbiased publications, such as travel guide booklets; the second are commercial sources, such as travel agents and their sales staff; the third are social sources, comprised of friends and relatives; the fourth are mass media, such as television, Internet, newspapers, and magazines (Luo, Feng, & Cai, 2004). In considering visiting a slow city, visitors use external sources such as media. Since slow city is a new concept, and many people have no internalized information about it, broadcast or published footage on the subject may create awareness which has the potential to reach visitors. Additionally, when the impact of the information obtained from social sources (friends and relatives) is considered, its influence on the potential visitor's choice of a slow city is more easily understood.

Decision Making

As decision making has the most complex structure in the consumer behavior model, the question of how to eliminate the barriers raised during this process merits further discussion. Even though there are many names or brands in a product set, visitors are expected to choose only one of these, or a selected few, within a limited time frame (Hana & Wozniak, 2001). Product sets which are not chosen will be lined up for other visitors. This is the case in tourism as well, where thousands of products (cities or resorts) are waiting for visitors (Kozak & Baloglu, 2010). However, in order to eliminate risk and to reach the targeted visitor group within the given time frame, service providers seek distinct solutions. One of the best examples of what is termed "product variety" is the slow city. Those cities which emphasize their assets in terms of their difference from other cities will be successful in gaining a high rank in the list of choices considered by potential visitors.

Experience

Experience is the time during which the visitors' expectations are realized, once they have successfully completed the decision making process and have purchased a product. We call this time frame in which visitors come together with the product and all the elements comprising the product (in other words, the time frame in which visitors live in the slow city) "experience" (Swarbrooke & Horner, 2001). At this stage, visitors' initial needs and the messages provided afterwards will have the most direct impact. During a holiday, visitors will refer to their initial expectations in the face of each experience and will want to test whether what was promised has been accomplished. This will determine the direction of how the visitors' quality of life or holiday is shaped. The quality factors involve the following: living in a slow city away from a crowded and hectic city life, awareness of more humane daily life which reflects the natural and cultural characteristics of the locality, and dishes prepared with natural products in accordance with the local style. These are the factors which visitors expect from a slow city and which help, in a general sense, to shape their holiday experience.

Post-Experience

The post-experience stage is the last stage of the visitor behavior model. At this stage, the influence of positive and negative personal experience on the visitors' final assessments is observed. This influence might emerge as a sense of satisfaction or dissatisfaction about the holiday spent in the city, and a positive or negative attitude or image of the city. As a result, these opinions will affect visitors' own future holiday plans and might affect other visitors' holiday plans as the result of the comments they make (Hyde, 2009). To some extent, while the experience of a slow city becomes an internal source of information for visitors' own future holiday plans, it also forms an internal source of information for others. As a whole, when taken as a tourism product, it is not possible to ignore the importance of influence of slow cities on visitor behavior.

METHOD

Interviews were conducted with 26 local visitors who visited Seferihisar between August 17 and August 20, 2012. These interviews lasted from 15 to 60 minutes. They were conducted in the areas of Sığacık and Akkum, which are popular tourist destinations. The visitors interviewed were selected from those who had stayed for a minimum of one night at any accommodation facility, and daily visitors were excluded. Interviews were conducted with the consent of the managers of the properties. During the interviews, only those visitors who volunteered and were familiar with the concept of the slow city were taken into consideration.

FINDINGS

Different professions are represented in the first group of participants, their age range was 34–68 years, and these visitors ranged from being on their first to their twentieth visit. The factors they gave for choosing to visit Seferihisar varied from its proximity to İzmir to the slow city aspect of the town. The composition of the sample was heterogeneous in terms of profession, age, frequency of visit, and purpose of visit. To ensure that the visitors were familiar with the meaning of slow city, all the respondents reported that they had already encountered the concept of slow city. However, a couple of respondents reported that they had realized what slow city meant only once they had come to Seferihisar, although they had heard the term previously. In such cases, people obtained first-hand information by experiencing the city themselves, rather than basing their information upon what they had been told:

> We came here from Istanbul and we didn't know what this concept meant. We thought it was a catchphrase of municipality. We noticed a snail symbol one week after we had arrived. Later, we realized that it connotated calmness, slowness. (Participant 1 – Public Relations)

Visitors seem to have the correct knowledge concerning the slow city. Some answers to questions concerning the nature of the slow city were as follows: sustaining city culture, preserving natural values, natural, calm, peaceful, an environmentally friendly approach instead of the hectic lifestyle caused by globalization, escape from the city, noise, and crowd, slow life, slow food, and slow work. In most explanations, slow city is associated with calm and silence. When all these contents are combined, the ingredients of the notion of slow city are completed.

Whether Seferihisar is a slow city does not have a significant impact on visitors' choice, because most have been here before. Thus, we can conclude that internal factors, such as previous personal experiences, have a greater influence on visitor behavior than external factors like brands or logos. However, the following quotations provide evidence that there are people whose next decision will be influenced by the awareness of the slow city concept, although they had previously visited Seferihisar:

> As we didn't know about slow city before we came, it didn't have any influence. However, it will affect our choice when we see another slow city and we will compare it to Seferihisar. (Participant 1 – Public Relations)

> We came here for the first time last year because it was a slow city. Being a slow city has influenced our decision this year again. (Participant 21 – Businessman)

> We accidentally learned that Seferihisar was a slow city when we first came. It was the reason for our next visit. (Participant 23 – Self-employed)

As these results show, the notion of slow city has an impact upon the first three stages of visitor behavior, namely needs awareness, information search and decision making, as well as an impact upon the post-consumption or repeat visit intentions at the fifth stage. Although it seems to have no impact on the first choice, any experience in the slow city is likely to affect the choice of destination and decision making for future holiday planning. As regards the holiday experience stage, visitors who had been to Seferihisar before observed the rapid pace of commercialization and an increase in visitor population. An increase in the number of visitors and vehicles has triggered a parking problem for vehicles.

> It was rather quiet before becoming a slow city. After being promoted by the media as a slow city, people who normally drive at 30 km/p started driving at 120 km/p. It has become overbuilt and almost lost its slow city character. Old traditional houses have been demolished and new ones have been built. Construction permits have been given in the protected areas. Ekmeksiz Beach has been closed. There is the problem of car park. (Participant 10 – Retired Businessman)

> Seferihisar used to be a peaceful place, but now we are not able to find a place to sit and we cannot park our cars in Sığacık. Landscaping is not adequate. Mostly middle aged and older people prefer to come here. (Participant 13 – Travel Agent)

Improvement in parks, planning and becoming slower are among the positive observations.

> Seferihisar has developed and become prettier since it became slow city. It used be like a village. Its landscape has improved. Especially Sığacık has developed a lot and become prettier. (Participant 8 – Worker)

However, the two quotations below are examples of both positive and negative observations.

> Traditional houses have been restored. There is great care on city planning. A marina is not a construction for a slow city, its previous state was more natural and beautiful; it has lost its character. (Participant 7 – Certified Public Accountant)

It used to be a slower city before it became a slow city, people were not eager to turn everything into cash. However, it would have been worse if it had not become a slow city. After becoming a slow city many more people arrived and this has stopped deterioration. (Participant 4 – Seaman)

While the sample destination has been able to preserve its traditional structure and revise its city planning, the controversial conclusion is that it has huge properties (a hotel, a marina, and a fish farm), it neglects the environment, the local people grew eager to turn what they own into cash, and migration has increased. In summary, visitors to Seferihisar are very reluctant in terms of slow city practices. While optimism about the protection of existing natural and cultural assets prevails, on the downside, it is doubted that the deterioring quality of life of local people and some uncontrollable developments resulting from tourism activities will bring various negative outcomes.

CONCLUSION AND IMPLICATIONS

First, slow city has an influence on visitors' needs and motivation to visit a destination. Second, visitors are likely to become familiar with slow city through their own personal experiences, even if they might have prior knowledge of the slow city concept from media or friends. Third, as slow city is a relatively new practice, it has some influence over visitors' need awareness and preferences for the existing and future decisions. Fourth, visitors have reported both positive impressions (landscaping, priority of culture, and nature) and negative impressions (crowd, car park, and commercialization, deterioration in natural and cultural values) of their personal experiences of a slow city. Visitors were also asked to compare their present and previous holidays in this respect. Finally, Seferihisar as a slow city may prevail over alternative destinations, after the information gained before, during, and after first-hand experience.

As a final remark, as with other similar studies, this research also has its particular limitations. First, the study is limited to a specific town in İzmir, Turkey, so that it can be applied at the national or international level, in order to make appropriate comparisons between study findings. In such a case, the study would include not only local visitor groups but also different visitor groups on an international vacation. Furthermore, a similar study could be conducted for local people on the demand side. Moreover, one could also follow the rule of participant observations as an alternative method, in order to reach more reliable conclusions.

REFERENCES

Engel, J. F., Blackwell, R. D., & Miniard, P. W. (1995). *Consumer behavior.* Fort Worth, TX: The Dryden Press.

Foodness, D., & Murray, B. (1999). A model of tourist information search behavior. *Journal of Travel Research, 37*(1), 220–230.

Hana, N., & Wozniak, R. (2001). *Consumer behavior: An applied approach.* Upper Saddle River, NJ: Prentice Hall.

Hyde, K. F. (2009). Tourist information search. In M. Kozak & A. Decrop (Eds.), *Handbook of tourist behavior* (pp. 50–64). New York, NY: Routledge.

Knox, P. L. (2005). Creating ordinary places: Slow cities in a fast world. *Journal of Urban Design, 10*(1), 1–11.

Kozak, M., & Baloglu, S. (2010). *Managing and marketing tourist destinations: Strategies to gain competitive edge.* New York, NY: Taylor & Francis.

Luo, M., Feng, R., & Cai, L. (2004). Information search behavior and tourist characteristics: The internet vis-à-vis other information sources. *Journal of Travel and Tourism Marketing, 17*(2/3), 15–25.

Mayer, H., & Knox, P. L. (2006). Slow cities: Sustainable places in a fast world. *Journal of Urban Affairs, 28*(4), 321–334.

Radstrom, S. (2005). *An urban identity movement rooted in the sustainable of place: A case study of slow cities and their application in rural Matinoba.* Master of City Planning, University of Manitoba, Department of City Planning.

Singh, S. (2012). Slow travel and Indian culture: Philosophical and practical aspects. In S. Fullagar, K. Markwell, & E. Wilson (Eds.), *Slow tourism: Experiences and mobilities* (pp. 214–226). Bristol: Channel View Publications.

Swarbrooke, J., & Horner, S. (2001). *Consumer behaviour in tourism.* Oxford: Heinemann.

A T-SHIRT FROM NEW YORK, A CORAL FROM MAURITIUS: A FUNCTIONAL TYPOLOGY OF TOURIST SOUVENIRS

Alain Decrop and Julie Masset

ABSTRACT

This chapter offers a deeper understanding of the symbols and meanings attached to tourists' special possessions as well as of the functions they fulfill in contemporary consumption. Nineteen informants have been interviewed and observed at home in a naturalistic interpretive perspective. Interview transcripts, field notes, and pictorial material were analyzed and interpreted through the grounded theory approach. This results in a new typology of symbolic souvenirs including touristic trinkets, destination stereotypes, paper mementoes, and picked-up objects. Such a typology relates to four major functions souvenirs may fulfill in terms of meanings and identity construction, that is, categorization, self-expression, connectedness, and self-creation.

Keywords: Tourist souvenirs; interpretive research; symbolic consumption; special possessions

Tourists' Behaviors and Evaluations
Advances in Culture, Tourism and Hospitality Research, Volume 9, 31–39
ISSN: 1871-3173/doi:10.1108/S1871-317320140000009003

INTRODUCTION

Shopping is one of the prevailing contemporary touristic rituals
— Belk (1997)

As underlined by Belk more than fifteen years ago, almost every consumer is involved in shopping activities while traveling or vacationing. Tourism shopping represents a major business for souvenir producers and retailers and so, for many tourism locations. According to the US Office of Travel and Tourism Industries, in 2011, 91.5% of all international leisure travelers are firstly interested in shopping (OTTI, 2011). Western tourists spend between 30% and 37% of their total travel budget on shopping whereas Asian tourists dedicate up to 61% of their budget to it (Timothy, 2005). Souvenirs and gifts constitute a significant part of tourist expenditures. For example, in 2011, 23.6% of the budget of international tourists visiting the United States was devoted to gifts and souvenirs while 25.2% and 19.7% was dedicated to lodging and food/beverages, respectively (OTTI, 2011).

In this study, we focus on material souvenirs, that is, all the objects that have been bought, picked up, or received at the vacation destination. We do not deal with the cognitive and affective memories, neither with the photographs taken during the holiday. More specifically, the study addresses the following research questions: What are the symbols and meanings associated with purchasing and consuming souvenirs? What roles/functions do souvenirs fulfill in postmodern consumption? This chapter contributes to a better knowledge of tourist souvenirs, a typical case of consumers' special possessions, which may be central in self-identity processes. Souvenirs are powerful "messengers of meaning" (Love & Sheldon, 1998) that help consumers to keep material connections with cherished past experiences and to give individual and social meanings to their broader existence.

THEORETICAL CONSIDERATIONS

Meanings of Special Possessions

People buy products not only for their functionalities but also for what they mean (Levy, 1959). As highlighted by Wallendorf, Belk, and Heisley (1988, p. 529), "informants often regarded some of their possessions as more than merely utilitarian things, that is, possessions held deep meanings in their lives." Consumers may be strongly attached to tourist souvenirs as well as to other cherished possessions such as a trophy won during a contest, a gift received from significant others, or a wedding ring. The meanings of special possessions mainly derive from symbolic person-, event-, or place-attachments rather than from utilitarian or hedonistic features. Belk (1988) adds that such deep meanings may result from a series of conditions associated with the object's acquisition (e.g., a pleasant travel experience, an achievement, a family heirloom). Furthermore, these special possessions may be a reflection of the person's self, of his/her identity (Belk, 1988; McCracken, 1988). In other words, possessions contribute to the definition of who we are (Csikszentmihalyi & Rochberg-Halton, 1981). Another potential source of these deep meanings is the sacred status conferred to these special possessions (Wallendorf et al., 1988). Finally, special household artifacts may offer to their owners a symbolic connection with their environment through a differentiation from others or an integration with others (Csikszentmihalyi & Rochberg-Halton, 1981). Valued possessions may emphasize the owner's individuality or express his/her integration with the social context.

Meanings of Souvenirs

(Some) tourist souvenirs are often regarded as special possessions to which consumers attach deep meanings (Belk, 1997; Wallendorf & Arnould, 1988). A few researchers already tried to understand the meanings attached to tourist souvenirs (Baker, Kleine, & Bowen, 2006; Decrop & Masset, 2011; Gordon, 1986; Littrell, 1990; Littrell, Anderson, & Brown, 1993; Love & Sheldon, 1998).

What we essentially know about souvenirs' meanings is that the profile of tourist consumers (e.g., shopping-oriented or authenticity seeking) and the level of tourists' experience (i.e., less experienced vs. more experienced travelers) affect the meanings assigned to souvenirs (Littrell, 1990; Love & Sheldon, 1998). Moreover, many layers of meanings exist and strong authenticity meanings are attached to souvenirs (Baker et al., 2006; Littrell et al., 1993). Finally, authors have attempted to develop typologies of souvenirs. Gordon (1986) was the first to publish such a typology including pictorial images, pieces-of-the-rock, symbolic shorthands, markers, and local products. She emphasizes the intrinsic characteristics of souvenirs and describes their functions as "a material reminder" and "a living messenger of the extraordinary." More recently, Decrop and Masset (2011) classified souvenirs according to four categories (i.e., symbolic, hedonistic, utilitarian, and the souvenir as a gift) based on the motivations of buying and consuming them.

METHOD

A naturalistic interpretive approach has been chosen to address our research questions (Lincoln & Guba, 1985). This type of approach aims to understand the occurrence of natural phenomena in their naturally occurring states. Geertz (1973) adds that immersing oneself in the field is needed to generate *thick descriptions*. We observed and discussed souvenirs in the temporal and spatial context of their acquisition and consumption.

Because we gave priority to information richness rather than to quantity or representativeness, we purposively selected our informants to maximize opportunities for theory development (Strauss & Corbin, 1990). Thirteen interviews were conducted involving 19 Belgian informants of different ages, genders, occupational positions, family compositions, and tourist involvements (i.e., the departure frequency per year).

In-depth interview, projective techniques, and participant observation were used in a triangulation perspective (Decrop, 1999). We also took photographs of our informants' vacation souvenirs in order to support our observation sessions. We used the grounded theory approach and a systematic coding scheme for analyzing and interpreting our interview transcripts, field notes, and pictorial material. In grounded theory, a local theory is built through an inductive analytical process rather than through a straight description of the data (Glaser & Strauss, 1967; Strauss & Corbin, 1990).

FINDINGS

When traveling or vacationing, almost every tourist buys or picks up a broad range of souvenirs, from commercial goods to objects picked up in the natural environment, to bring back in the home country. A new typology emerged from data analysis, which includes four types of symbolic souvenirs: touristic trinkets, destination stereotypes, paper mementoes, and picked-up objects. Our typology is grounded on four major functions souvenirs may fulfill in terms of consumers' meanings and identity construction,

		Meaning derives from	
		Culture	Individual
Souvenir helps define the consumer as	A member of a group (tourist subculture)	*1. Touristic trinkets* Categorization function	*3. Paper mementoes* Connectedness function
	An individual (a singular tourist)	*2. Destination stereotypes* Self-expression function	*4. Picked-up objects* Self-creation function

Fig. 1. Types and Functions of Symbolic Souvenirs.

that is: categorization, self-expression, connectedness, and self-creation. Of course, not all souvenirs are symbolic. Some of them only fulfill utilitarian or hedonistic functions but such souvenirs were not considered in our study.

Fig. 1 presents the four types of symbolic souvenirs and their respective functions. It is inspired by the two dimensions of symbolic consumer behavior suggested by Hoyer and MacInnis (2004).

The first (horizontal) dimension stands for the source of meanings given to souvenirs, that is, cultural versus personal. Either cultural/public meanings or personal/private meanings can be assigned to tourists' possessions. The second (vertical) dimension related to the role of souvenirs in identity construction, that is, collective versus individual. Souvenirs can help the tourist to define or to assert him/herself as a member of a group or of the tourist subculture as well as an individual or a singular tourist.

Touristic Trinkets: Categorization

Touristic trinkets include small trinkets or gadgets (e.g., mugs, key rings, T-shirts) that feature the visited place(s). They are cheap and bought in souvenir shops during each holiday. These trinkets often fulfill an emblematic or categorization function. Public meanings are given to these souvenirs printed with the name or a drawing of the destination. For instance, when seeing someone's wearing a T-shirt with palm trees and printed with "Republica Dominicana," the majority of people are going to conclude that he/she visited the Dominican Republic.

In addition, tourist consumers buy and use these objects to symbolize their belonging to a group of travelers or to the broader tourist subculture. Informants express this need of integration in those words: *"We are sometimes encouraged to buy. When we went to Gibraltar, we were in a package tour by bus. When we got off the bus, a guy took pictures of each tourist. At the end of the tour, the same guy proposed us key rings and ashtrays with a photo of Gibraltar and us. Almost every tourist bought this souvenir. We bought a key ring. Actually, we were conduced to buy it because everybody stayed to buy one ... so, we bought one too"* (*Renée and Willy, F/M, 50/50*).

Destination Stereotypes: Self-Expression

Destination stereotypes are typical objects from the destination described as *the speciality of the place* (e.g., Russian dolls, Egyptian papyrus). Although informants are aware that these objects are not unique and are mass-produced, they still buy them because they represent the destination.

These souvenirs serve ego-enhancement and self-expression functions. On the one hand, public meanings deriving from culture are given to these objects. For example, the majority of people know that the Eiffel Tower belongs to Paris. On the other hand, these souvenirs help the consumer to distinguish him/herself from a group or the tourist subculture and so, to define him/herself as an individual as the following informant underlines: *"The person who went there [New York], he/she must think that the Statue of Liberty is a souvenir for him/her. But I have the feeling that it is more to communicate to others 'I went to New York'"* (*Frédérique, F, 27*). Destination stereotypes are often conspicuously exhibited in the public rooms of the house (e.g., living-room) to show to visiting friends and relatives that "I/we was/were there."

Paper Mementoes: Connectedness

The third category of souvenirs, that is, paper mementoes, includes collector items such as entrance tickets, guidebooks, trip brochures, city maps, and flight/luggage tickets. This type of souvenirs clearly fulfills a connectedness function. Symbolizing the personal connections with relevant people, events, or experiences in the tourist's life, these souvenirs are imbued with personal and private meanings. For example, some people keep the flight tickets of their honeymoon or of their first air travel.

Furthermore, paper mementoes represent the tourist's affiliation with a group of travelers. The following informant tends to manifest, through her guidebook, her membership to the group of former teachers traveling with her: *"The friend who organized the trip, she knew all the participants, and it is always well prepared because ... Look, she made us a guidebook with all the things that we were going to see and the description of these. Because the group was made of former teachers like me and we like to know where we go and to set up all the details"* (*Yvette, F, 63*).

Picked-Up Objects: Self-Creation

Informants mention the fourth type of souvenirs with the highest enthusiasm, that is, picked-up objects such as stones, sand, coral, and lavender. Picked-up objects contribute to self-creation. Private meanings derive from those objects as their signification is only obvious for the tourist who brought them back. Most often, these souvenirs are associated with significant personal events, anecdotes, or experiences. For example, a coral brought back from Mauritius is only unique and distinctive for his/her owner because it was received from a local. For outsiders, it is just something inexpensive, ordinary, and usual. An affective or symbolic value rather than an economic one is attached to such souvenirs.

Moreover, these picked-up objects help the tourist to stand out from others and to affirm his/her uniqueness and individuality as expressed by one of our informants: *"Maybe everyone can bring a stone from the Statue of Liberty, but this one, I picked it up myself. This stone is just a stone ... But I wanted to bring a piece of the United States back home. It does not have [an economic value] but for me, it means that I have at home something from the United States"* (*Jean-Claude, M, 56*).

Tourists especially cherish picked-up objects because they have been symbolically contaminated (Belk, 1988; Belk, Wallendorf, & Sherry, 1991) as illustrated by the previous quote in which the stone is imbued with the Statue of Liberty. These souvenirs are often separated from profane spaces and displayed in more private/sacred rooms of the house (e.g., bedrooms, office) in order to keep or reinforce their sacred status.

CONCLUSION AND IMPLICATIONS

In this chapter, we strove to better and deeply understand the symbols and meanings attached to tourist souvenirs and the functions they fulfill in contemporary consumption. Souvenirs exist for a long time and will continue to be a crucial part of the touristic experience as long as people continue to travel. The typology presented in this chapter contributes to the field of consumers' special possessions by highlighting the role of souvenirs in self-identity processes. The meanings inherent to picked-up objects and destination stereotypes are in line with the extended-self concept (Belk, 1988). Because of their association with a personal meaningful event or story and thus, because of their participation in the definition of the tourist's identity, picked-up objects are incorporated in the tourist's self. In the same way, destination stereotypes support the tourist's self-expression when the tourist presents the speciality of the place to others and, consequently, asserts his/her presence at the destination.

Our study adds depth to souvenir research. In contrast with many previous studies, we considered both the functional and symbolic dimensions of tourist souvenirs and provided a better and in-depth understanding through a naturalistic interpretive approach. By interviewing tourists and observing their souvenirs in their full home context, we were also able to propose a richer and deeper comprehension of these possessions. Typologies such as the one proposed in this chapter are essential not only for researchers but also for marketers and retailers (Swanson & Timothy, 2012). They help them structure their thoughts and theories, better understand the market, and implement their merchandising strategies (Swanson & Timothy, 2012). For example, our typology could help souvenir producers and retailers to adapt their offering and so, to develop distinctive souvenirs that draw tourists' attention. However, our typology is not mutually exclusive as the same souvenir can fulfill several functions at the same time. Moreover, it would be interesting to take cultural differences into account as our sample is only composed of Belgian informants.

REFERENCES

Baker, S. M., Kleine, S. S., & Bowen, H. E. (2006). On the symbolic meaning of souvenirs for children. *Research in Consumer Behavior, 10*, 213–252.

Belk, R. W. (1988). Possessions and the extended self. *Journal of Consumer Research, 15*(2), 139–168.

Belk, R. W. (1997). Been there, done that, bought the souvenirs: Of journeys and boundary crossing. In S. Brown & D. Turley (Eds.), *Consumer research: Postcards from the edge* (pp. 22–45). London: Routledge.

Belk, R. W., Wallendorf, M., & Sherry, J. F., Jr. (1991). The sacred and the profane in consumer behavior: Theodicy on the Odyssey. In R. W. Belk (Ed.), *Highways and buyways: Naturalistic research from the consumer behavior Odyssey* (pp. 59–101). Provo, UT: Association for Consumer Research.

Csikszentmihalyi, M., & Rochberg-Halton, E. (1981). *The meaning of things: Domestic symbols and the self.* Cambridge: Cambridge University Press.

Decrop, A. (1999). Triangulation in qualitative tourism research. *Tourism Management, 20*(1), 157–161.

Decrop, A., & Masset, J. (2011). I want this Ramses' statue: Motives and meanings of tourist souvenirs. In M. Kozak & N. Kozak (Eds.), *Sustainability of tourism: Cultural and environmental perspectives* (pp. 17–41). UK: Cambridge Scholars Publishing.

Geertz, C. (1973). Deep play: Notes on the Balinese cockfight. In C. Geertz (Ed.), *The interpretation of cultures* (pp. 412–453). New York, NY: Basic Books.

Glaser, B. G., & Strauss, A. S. (1967). *The discovery of grounded theory: Strategies for qualitative research.* Chicago, IL: Aldine.

Gordon, B. (1986). The souvenir: Messenger of the extraordinary. *Journal of Popular Culture, 20*(3), 135–146.

Hoyer, W. D., & MacInnis, D. J. (2004). *Consumer behavior* (3rd ed.). Boston, MA: Houghton Mifflin Company.

Levy, S. J. (1959). Symbols for sale. *Harvard Business Review, 37*(4), 117–124.

Lincoln, Y. S., & Guba, E. G. (1985). *Naturalistic inquiry.* Beverly Hills, CA: Sage.

Littrell, M. A. (1990). Symbolic significance of textile crafts for tourists. *Annals of Tourism Research, 17*(2), 228–245.

Littrell, M. A., Anderson, L. F., & Brown, P. J. (1993). What makes a craft souvenir authentic? *Annals of Tourism Research, 20*(1), 197–215.

Love, L. L., & Sheldon, P. S. (1998). Souvenirs: Messengers of meaning. In J. W. Alba & J. Wesley (Eds.), *Advances in consumer research* (Vol. 25, pp. 170–175). Provo, UT: Association for Consumer Research.

McCracken, G. (1988). *Culture and consumption: New approaches to the symbolic character of consumption goods and activities.* Bloomington, IN: Indiana University Press.

OTTI (Office of Travel and Tourism Industries). (2011). *Profiles of overseas travelers to the United States: 2011 inbound.* Retrieved from http://tinet.ita.doc.gov/outreachpages/inbound.general_information.inbound_overview.html

Strauss, A. L., & Corbin, J. (1990). *Basics of qualitative research: Grounded theory procedures and techniques.* Newbury Park, CA: Sage.

Swanson, K. K., & Timothy, D. J. (2012). Souvenirs: Icons of meaning, commercialization and commoditization. *Tourism Management, 33*(3), 489–499.

Timothy, D. J. (2005). *Shopping tourism, retailing, and leisure.* Clevedon: Channel View Publications.

Wallendorf, M., & Arnould, E. J. (1988). My favorite things: A cross-cultural inquiry into object attachment, possessiveness, and social linkage. *Journal of Consumer Research, 14*(4), 531–547.

Wallendorf, M., Belk, R. W., & Heisley, D. (1988). Deep meaning in possessions: The paper. In M. J. Houston (Ed.), *Advances in consumer research* (Vol. 15, pp. 528–530). Provo, UT: Association for Consumer Research.

EXHIBITION AREAS: CASE STUDY RESEARCH OF JAPANESE FIRMS

Yosuke Endo, Yohei Kurata and Taketo Naoi

ABSTRACT

This chapter presents the potential of exhibition areas operated by consumer goods companies as a method of relationship marketing for corporate branding. Exhibition areas can provide visitors with opportunities to understand corporate brands. In order to clarify the roles of exhibition areas in corporate strategies, we conducted enterprise investigations of three Japanese companies, Sony, Nikka Whisky, and Toyota. Although we would like to propose that operating exhibition areas might be effective for marketing, the results show some differences among the companies in visitors' data and their purposes. We should first question whether this method is suitable for each company in consideration of their view of corporate branding.

Keywords: Corporate branding; exhibition areas; relationship marketing

Tourists' Behaviors and Evaluations
Advances in Culture, Tourism and Hospitality Research, Volume 9, 41–48
Copyright © 2014 by Emerald Group Publishing Limited
All rights of reproduction in any form reserved
ISSN: 1871-3173/doi:10.1108/S1871-317320140000009004

INTRODUCTION

This study focuses on corporate activities of building relationships with customers with the use of exhibition areas. Company's showrooms, for example, provide visitors with opportunities to be informed of their products and corporate brands by direct communication such as Sony Building (Fig. 1). As Sheth and Parvatiyar (2002) claim in the field of marketing, strong relationships with customers can help companies to project their impressive brand images in customers' minds and, in so doing, strengthen customer loyalty.

In recent years, establishment of a corporate brand has been a crucial issue for the Japanese industry, especially consumer goods companies (Ministry of Economy, Trade and Industry, 2012). Indeed, the Japanese government embarked on a strategy to develop the tourism industry not only for Japan's economic propensity but also for reinforcement of its soft power in the world market (Japan Tourism Agency, 2010). Soft power is defined as a favorable image and impression of a country which foreigners have (McGray, 2002). From a similar perspective, Erickson, Johansson, and Chao (1984) terms products' values added by a country brand, country-of-origin effects.

Fig. 1.   Sony Building in Tokyo.

Our opinion is that country-of-origin effects may explain possible relationships between tourists and country brands. Evaluating the relevance
among tourism and country brands, Gnoth (2002) suggests that we should
explore the links between tourists' experience and export products. In terms
of Gnoth's contention, we suppose that consumers may associate consumer
goods brands with country brands and places where they have been
produced.

We thus regard corporate brands of domestic firms as a measure to
foster inbound tourism. Customers who are loyal to a certain brand may
wish to visit the country of its brand's origin. Such a notion is particularly
important in Japan, which is considered as a manufacturing country and is
currently aiming to foster its tourism industry. In addition, if more overseas
tourists come to Japan, Japanese consumer goods companies will have
more chances to communicate directly with the tourists.

In this chapter, we have studied exhibition areas operated by consumer
goods companies in Japan. We presented three examples of Japanese
companies, Sony, Nikka Whisky and Toyota. These companies provide
opportunities for visitors to communicate directly with their products in
their exhibition areas. For the data collection, we conducted a questionnaire
survey to the three companies. On the basis of the results, we identified
the present situations of the three Japanese companies and their current
operation of their exhibition areas, and discuss the roles of the exhibition
areas in the companies' marketing strategies.

THEORETICAL CONSIDERATIONS

Consumer goods companies have several places where customers are able
to come in touch with their products or services, and we define such places
as exhibition areas in this study. Many of them have showrooms and store
buildings, and factory tours are operated. Some researchers have also
studied such facilities in the field of marketing.

Walvis (2004) calls corporate symbolic sites that can be used as communication platforms for customers, brand locations. Brand locations include
manufacturers' facilities as well as non-manufacturers' facilities, such as
Disneyland, which is operated by an entertainment company, Walt Disney.
German car manufacturer, for example, have operated their automobile
museums such as Mercedes-Benz Museum, Porsche Museum, and BMW
Welt. These museums have showrooms and exhibitions in an attempt to

offer information about the companies (Coles & Hall, 2008). Therefore, we can consider exhibition areas of consumer goods companies as parts of brand locations.

Similarly, Kent and Brown (2009) points out the importance of flagship stores for retail companies. Flagship stores are placed as the core store of retail chains and often located in capital cities. In comparison with standard stores, flagship stores function as advertisement to raise awareness of customers and reinforce retail brands. The Louis Vuitton, for example, has a flagship store in the Champs Elysee in Paris, which is a popular tourism destination (Louis Vuitton, 2013). Such a firm may have intention to enhance their brand images through communication with tourists at its flag store.

This study also refers to customer relationship marketing, which means a marketing method to build relationships with customers (Stone, Woodcock, & Machtynger, 1995). This term has been used and defined by many managers and marketers in different ways, and is often regarded as a method for companies to retain customers' information with the use of e-commerce technologies (Foss & Stone, 2001). In this chapter, however, we consider this concept to cover a broader range of marketing methods to manage relationships with customers, and we regard operating exhibition areas as one of the methods of customer relationship marketing in that they function as platforms to communicate directly with customers.

METHOD

We conducted questionnaire surveys to three Japanese companies so as to clarify the present situations of their exhibition areas. The First case is Sony, which is a consumer electronics company and has a flagship store, Sony Building, in Tokyo. Nikka Whisky is the second case and this firm is a subsidiary company of Asahi group which produces beverages and alcoholic drinks. Nikka Whisky operates factory tours at their distilleries, and visitors can observe the process of producing Japanese whisky and taste Nikka's original whisky. The third case is Toyota which produces and sells automobile products all over the world and this company operates factory tours at their exhibition areas, Toyota Kaikan Exhibition Hall. This exhibition facility is located in the place where Toyota was founded, and the headquarters is located in the same place. We sent out questionnaires to the three companies. The questionnaire has three sections: visitors' data of the exhibition areas in 2010, the purpose of operating exhibition areas, and the exhibition areas' relevance to the company's strategy.

FINDINGS

Sony Building is in a luxury shopping district in Tokyo, and visitors have opportunities to try out electronic appliances and purchase products in the showroom. Additionally, the Customer Information Counter provides visitors with an opportunity for interactive communication with the working staffs who offer advice on how to use Sony's products (Sony Building, 2013). According to Sony's answer to our questionnaire, Sony Building attracted about 4,500,000 visitors in 2010, and most of them were tourist groups. The main purpose of operating Sony Building is to promote their products and to enhance its corporate brand image. This facility is supervised by the brand management division of Sony's headquarters, and their answers to our questionnaire were provided under the name of Sony Network Communication Service in Branding Site Management. Sony appears to regard the operation of the exhibition areas as part of their branding strategy.

Nikka Whisky is the second example and their products have won several prizes in the World Whisky Award in recent years (Nikka Whisky, 2013). This firm arranges factory tours in two producing areas: the whisky distilleries in Miyagi Prefecture and Hokkaido Prefecture in Japan. The two distilleries have several facilities for factory tours: exhibitions and a shopping area. Visitors are able to observe the producing process of Nikka Whisky and taste and buy their products during the factory tours (Nikka Whisky Distilleries, 2013). According to Nikka's answers to our questionnaire, the Miyagi distillery attracted about 184,000 annual visitors, while 252,009 people visited the Yoichi distillery in 2010. Furthermore, these distilleries cooperate with travel agents in order to increase the number of tourists. Probably as the result, tourist groups were the major segment of visitors in both the distilleries. With reference to these pieces of information, we consider that Nikka Whisky aims to leverage its products as the means to communicate with customers in its productive areas. The sales department of Nikka Whisky answered to all of the questions. Beverland (2009) proposes that originality and authenticity are important elements for brand management of products. MacCannell (1999) also has claimed that tourists wish to understand the authenticity of tourism destination, and the authenticity of a thing tends to be associated with the place of its origin. Thus, we suppose that Nikka's factory tours may be an effective way of corporate branding in that visitors are offered a chance to sense the brand originality of Nikka with explanations about the manufacturing process.

The third case, Toyota, is a Japanese automobile company that has been expanding its business throughout the world (Toyota Annual Report, 2012). The headquarters of Toyota is in Aichi Prefecture in Japan. Their corporate museum Toyota Kaikan Exhibition Hall is located in the same place, and factory tours are also operated. The facility has some exhibitions about advanced technologies and the corporate history of Toyota. According to the response to our questionnaire by Toyota Citizenship Division, this facility attracted about 320,000 visitors in 2010, and student groups were the major segment. The most important and interesting fact is that Toyota does not manage this facility for marketing nor corporate branding, and the purpose is social contributions to the surrounding areas of the factory. Student groups, who are the main segment, are not likely to purchase Toyota's products soon after their visit to the facility, but may become potential customers in the future. According to the theory of relationship marketing, however, maintenance of relationships with the existing customers is more important for companies than acquiring new customers (Berry, 2002). Therefore, we consider that Toyota does not operate this corporate museum as part of its strategy of customer relationship marketing, unlike the other cases, Sony Building and Nikka Whisky Distilleries.

The results of surveys show some differences among three companies in current situations of operating their exhibition areas (Table 1). Although we presumed that operating exhibition areas should be regarded as part of customer relationship marketing, the results suggested that such a notion is not necessarily shared by every sort of companies. As long as we have

Table 1.   Visitors Data in 2010 and Purpose of Operating Exhibition Areas.

	Annual Visitors	Most Visitors	Purpose and Strategy
Sony Building	4,500,000	Tourist groups	Advertisement and Corporate Branding
Nikka Whisky distillery tours	252,009 (Yoichi) 184,000 (Miyagi)	Tourist groups	Advertisement and Corporate Branding
Toyota Exhibition Hall and factory tours	320,000	Student groups	Social contributions

observed the cases of Sony and Nikka Whisky, their exhibition areas are operated as a means for corporate branding and relationship marketing. Contrary to our expectation, however, Toyota is clearly different from the other two cases in light of their purpose and the main target of attracting visitors.

CONCLUSION AND IMPLICATIONS

Establishment of brand images is an important issue for the Japanese industry. Porter, Takeuchi, and Sakakibara (2000) points out that Japanese companies have remarkable abilities of production, but that they are not good at fostering customers' understanding of the originality of their products compared to their overseas competitors. As one of the solutions for this problem, we proposed the method of operating exhibition areas as a customer relationship marketing strategy. Operation of exhibition areas may be an effective way for a company to communicate with their customers, possibly including tourists, and make them realize the essence of the brands' originality. On account of the above results and observations concerning the three Japanese companies, however, the roles of exhibition areas are implied to vary depending on corporate strategies of respective companies. In view of opportunities to attract a large number of visitors, we suppose, urban areas are more suitable as locations for exhibition areas than their producing sites like Sony Building, and, while some companies like Nikka Whisky may put emphasis on their brands' originality related to their producing areas, others, such as Toyota, may choose locations that are suitable to attract visitors.

In order to develop this method, consumer goods companies should understand how their brand's originality relates to the producing place, which can also be used as their exhibition areas from the perspectives of customers, and future studies need to investigate consumers' perceptions of corporate brand originality and authenticity as related to producing places.

ACKNOWLEDGMENT

The authors appreciate the comments and helpful advice from Juergen Gnoth, Otago University, to this study.

REFERENCES

Berry, L. L. (2002). Relationship marketing of services-perspectives from 1983 and 2000. *Journal of Relationship Marketing, 1*(1), 59−77.

Beverland, M. B. (2009). *Building brand authenticity: 7 habits of iconic brands.* New York, NY: Palgrave Macmillan.

Coles, T., & Hall, C. M. (2008). *International business and tourism: Global issues, contemporary interactions.* New York, NY: Routledge.

Erickson, G. M., Johansson, J. K., & Chao, P. (1984). Image variables in multi-attribute product evaluations: Country-of-origin effects. *The Journal of Consumer Research, 11*(2), 694−699.

Foss, B., & Stone, M. (2001). *Successful customer relationship marketing: New thinking, new strategies, new tools, for getting closer to your customers.* London: Kogan Page.

Gnoth, J. (2002). Leveraging export brands through a tourism destination brand. *Journal of Brand Management, 9*(4), 262−280.

Japan Tourism Agency. (2010). Building a tourism nation. *Retrieved from* https://www.mlit.go.jp/common/000060096.pdf

Kent, T., & Brown, R. (2009). *Flagship marketing: Concepts and places.* London: Routledge.

Louis Vuitton. (2013). *Homepage.* Retrieved from http://www.louisvuitton.fr/front/#/fra_FR/Homepage

MacCannell, D. (1999). *The tourist: A new theory of the leisure class.* Berkeley and Los Angele: University of California Press.

McGray, D. (2002). Japan's gross national cool. *Foreign Policy, 130,* 44−54.

Ministry of Economy, Trade and Industry. (2012). The white paper on manufacturing industry. *Retrieved from* http://www.meti.go.jp/report/whitepaper/mono/2012/pdf/honbun02_01_08.pdf

Nikka Whisky. (2013). *Homepage.* Retrieved from http://www.nikka.com/eng/award/index.html

Nikka Whisky Distilleries. (2013). *Homepage.* Retrieved from http://www.nikka.com/eng/distilleries/index.html

Porter, M., Takeuchi, H., & Sakakibara, M. (2000). *Can Japan compete?* New York, NY: Basic Books.

Sheth, J. N., & Parvatiyar, A. (2002). Evolving relationship marketing into a discipline. *Journal of Relationship Marketing, 1*(1), 3−16.

Sony Building. (2013). *Homepage.* Retrieved from http://www.sonybuilding.jp/e/index.html

Stone, M., Woodcock, N., & Machtynger, L. (1995). *Customer relationship marketing: Get to know your customers and win their loyalty.* London: Kogan Page.

Toyota Annual Report. (2012). Retrieved from http://www.toyota-global.com/investors/ir_library/annual/pdf/2012/

Walvis, T. (2004). Building bland locations. *Corporate Reputation Review, 5*(4), 358−366.

INDIVIDUAL VALUES AND HOLIDAY PREFERENCES

Tamara Jovanovic

ABSTRACT

This chapter aims to explore relationship between individual values and holiday preferences. Values as standards of assessing behaviors are often used in tourism research and have been connected to tourists' behaviors and activities preferences. In this chapter, Schwartz Value Survey (Schwartz, 1992) was used to determine individual values. Holiday preferences were evaluated on a Likert scale using two separate lists: types of destination (e.g., seaside, city) and forms of holiday (e.g., local, short). Sample consisted of 120 university students in Serbia. Results show that there is a correlation between values and holiday preferences. Implications are further discussed in the chapter.

Keywords: Individual values; holiday preferences; correlation; Serbia

INTRODUCTION

The assumption of this research is that since values influence activities they should also influence holiday preferences because they imply different possible activities and goals that can be achieved on that holiday. People

Tourists' Behaviors and Evaluations
Advances in Culture, Tourism and Hospitality Research, Volume 9, 49–57
Copyright © 2014 by Emerald Group Publishing Limited
All rights of reproduction in any form reserved
ISSN: 1871-3173/doi:10.1108/S1871-317320140000009005

travel to different destinations with the expectations of what those destinations have to offer. Also, people choose how a holiday is going to look like, is it going to be short or long, will they travel individually or in groups, depending on their plans of behavior on that destination.

THEORETICAL CONSIDERATIONS

Values represent concepts or beliefs about life and desirable behavior (Jago, 1997). They go beyond specific situations and guide the process of selection and evaluation of behaviors or events (Schwartz, 1992). They are more stabile over time than attitudes and many authors claim that they are an important part of personality (Crick-Furman & Prentice, 2000; Madrigal & Kahle, 1994; McCleary & Choi, 1999; Muller, 1991; Pitts & Woodside, 1986; Schwartz, 1992).

Schwartz and Bilsky (1987) offered eight basic value (motivation) domains but later (Schwartz, 1992) this list was extended into 11 value domains (see "Method" section). Ten of these value domains have been conceptually distinguished and empirically identified in a multitude of cross-cultural samples (Schwartz, 1994; Schwartz & Sagiv, 1995). However, Spirituality has not had a consistent broad meaning in cross-cultural studies and Schwartz (1994) has excluded this value domain; he deemed it near-universal, even though ultimate meaning in life has been shown to be a distinct and basic human need (Schwartz, 1992). In this research, older model with 11 value domains has been used since it is our belief that Spirituality is a value domain of significance and should not be excluded from the research.

Researchers have been exploring the influence of individual values on tourism behavior (Backman & Crompton, 1990; Beatty, Kahle, Homer, & Mirsa, 1985). Studies have shown that values influence the choice of holiday destination and activities during holiday (Beatty, Kahle, & Homer, 1991; Jackson, 1973; Morrison, Hsieh, & O'Leary, 1994). Values have been proven useful in marketing of tourist offers – while developing the product and in marketing strategies (Muller, 1991; Pitts & Woodside, 1986). They have also been connected with the preferences of certain holiday activities (Beatty et al., 1985; Crick-Furman & Prentice, 2000; Madrigal & Kahle, 1994; Muller, 1991; Pitts & Woodside, 1986). However, there are no available studies that directly explore relationship between values and holiday preferences – types of destination (e.g., seaside, mountains) and forms of holiday (e.g., individual, mass).

METHOD

Respondents of this study were 120 students of the Faculty of Sciences, University of Novi Sad, Serbia. They were mostly female (73%), aged from 19 to 26 (95%).

Questionnaire used in this study consisted of three parts. First part measured socio-demographic characteristics of the respondents: gender, age, place of residence, and marital status.

Second part measured with Likert scale (1–7) holiday preferences which were divided into two lists: type of destination and form of holiday. List *type of destination* consisted of seven most popular types of destination in Serbia (Jovanovic, Majstorovic, Dinic, & Armenski, 2012): seaside, mountain, city, spa, village, river, lake. List *form of holiday* included eight categories that can describe one's holiday: abroad, local, long, short, mass, individual, active, relaxation.

Third part of the questionnaire measured individual values using Schwartz Value Survey (SVS) (Schwartz, 1992). SVS consists of 56 items, 30 terminal and 26 instrumental values. These items measure 11 value domains: Spirituality (4 items), Achievement (6), Self-direction (6), Hedonism (3), Security (7), Tradition (5), Universalism (7), Benevolence (7), Conformity (4), Stimulation (3), and Power (4). Importance of each value as a guiding principle in respondents life is assessed on the 9-point scale, labeled: 7 (of supreme importance), 6 (very important), 5, 4 (unlabeled), 3 (important), 2, 1 (unlabeled), 0 (not important), −1 (opposed to my values). Unlike other typical scales, this scale enables respondents to express opposition to certain values. Reliability of each value domain ranges from $\alpha = 0.61$ for Tradition to $\alpha = 0.75$ for Universalism.

FINDINGS

Analyses were conducted using SPSS 17.0. Value domains were calculated by averaging scores on each of the corresponding items in SVS. Pearson's correlation between value domains and holiday preferences was calculated. Table 1 shows correlation between types of destinations and value domains. All correlations are with coefficients between $r = 0.185$ and $r = 0.312$, which are not high but still statistically significant ($p < 0.05$).

Tourists that prefer the *seaside* as destination have high achievement and security values. Those who prefer *mountains* highly value benevolence

Table 1.   Correlations between Individual Values and Types of
Destinations.

		Seaside	Mountain	City	Spa	Village	River	Lake
Benevolence	r	0.156	0.214*	0.045	0.17	0.212*	0.270**	0.208*
	p	0.09	0.019	0.625	0.064	0.02	0.003	0.023
Universalism	r	−0.003	0.206*	0.109	0.17	0.185*	0.312**	0.324**
	p	0.973	0.024	0.235	0.064	0.043	0.001	0.000
Self-direction	r	0.12	0.012	0.027	0.027	0.065	0.186*	0.253**
	p	0.19	0.899	0.767	0.768	0.48	0.042	0.005
Stimulation	r	0.083	0.059	0.225*	0.07	0.05	0.211*	0.156
	p	0.369	0.524	0.014	0.446	0.591	0.021	0.089
Hedonism	r	0.148	−0.132	0.045	−0.034	0.033	−0.072	−0.079
	p	0.107	0.149	0.626	0.714	0.719	0.432	0.39
Achievement	r	0.241**	0.031	0.152	0.055	−0.069	0.157	0.148
	p	0.008	0.736	0.097	0.552	0.454	0.086	0.107
Power	r	0.117	−0.002	0.203*	0.057	0.039	0.119	0.06
	p	0.202	0.981	0.027	0.537	0.669	0.195	0.515
Security	r	0.200*	0.06	0.135	0.113	−0.007	0.145	0.074
	p	0.028	0.518	0.141	0.217	0.942	0.115	0.425
Tradition	r	0.055	0.089	−0.031	0.141	0.249**	0.238**	0.124
	p	0.549	0.333	0.739	0.125	0.006	0.009	0.176
Conformity	r	0.037	0.075	0.01	0.126	0.004	0.083	0.1
	p	0.692	0.415	0.915	0.17	0.969	0.367	0.278
Spirituality	r	0.025	0.119	0.038	0.007	0.043	0.207*	0.223*
	p	0.783	0.194	0.678	0.938	0.642	0.023	0.014

*significance at the level of $p < 0.05$.
**significance at the level of $p < 0.01$.

and universalism. *City* as destination attracts tourists who value stimulation and power. *Spas* have only marginally significant correlations with
benevolence and universalism. *Villages* are popular with people that have
high benevolence, universalism, and tradition values. Tourists that prefer
rivers value benevolence, universalism, self-direction, stimulation, spirituality, and tradition. *Lakes* have similar relationship with values as rivers but
without significant correlations with tradition and stimulation values.

Relationship between individual values and forms of holiday can be seen
in Table 2. Significant correlation coefficients vary between $r = 0.181$ and
$r = 0.463$. People who prefer to travel *abroad* value benevolence, universalism, stimulation, and achievement. Those who like to touristically visit
local destinations have high benevolence, universalism, and tradition
values. *Longer* holiday is attractive for those who value benevolence, universalism, self-direction, stimulation, and achievement. Tourists who prefer

Table 2. Correlations between Individual Values and Forms of Holiday.

		Abroad	Local	Long	Short	Mass	Individual	Active	Relaxation
Benevolence	r	0.213*	0.326**	0.256**	0.236**	0.105	0.054	0.201*	0.089
	p	0.02	0.000	0.005	0.01	0.253	0.561	0.028	0.335
Universalism	r	0.204*	0.206*	0.209*	0.129	0.06	0.024	0.271**	-0.009
	p	0.026	0.024	0.022	0.162	0.517	0.796	0.003	0.923
Self-direction	r	0.11	0.035	0.247**	0.111	0.126	0.047	0.361**	-0.039
	p	0.231	0.702	0.006	0.229	0.171	0.608	0.000	0.669
Stimulation	r	0.208*	-0.052	0.349**	-0.102	0.303**	-0.005	0.381**	0.115
	p	0.023	0.572	0.000	0.266	0.001	0.959	0.000	0.211
Hedonism	r	-0.003	-0.103	0.157	-0.084	0.181*	-0.213*	0.171	0.185*
	p	0.975	0.262	0.087	0.362	0.048	0.019	0.062	0.043
Achievement	r	0.269**	-0.022	0.278**	-0.046	0.156	0.052	0.463**	0.093
	p	0.003	0.814	0.002	0.617	0.089	0.571	0.000	0.311
Power	r	0.107	0.021	0.178	-0.106	0.162	-0.117	0.244**	0.185*
	p	0.246	0.817	0.052	0.25	0.077	0.203	0.007	0.043
Security	r	0.152	0.074	0.052	0.11	0.007	-0.001	0.179	0.138
	p	0.098	0.425	0.134	0.23	0.942	0.991	0.05	0.132
Tradition	r	0.105	0.208*	0.145	0.09	-0.005	0.008	0.06	0.099
	p	0.255	0.023	0.139	0.326	0.954	0.927	0.513	0.281
Conformity	r	0.091	0.169	0.104	0.135	-0.048	0.103	0.14	0.027
	p	0.322	0.064	0.26	0.141	0.602	0.264	0.128	0.769
Spirituality	r	0.08	0.086	0.157	0.114	-0.055	0.144	0.059	0.037
	p	0.387	0.349	0.087	0.213	0.55	0.117	0.522	0.685

*significance at the level of $p < 0.05$.
**significance at the level of $p < 0.01$.

short holiday value benevolence. *Mass* holiday is for those who have high stimulation and hedonism. *Active* holiday has a similar relationship with values as the form of long holiday except that it also correlates with power. Tourists who search *relaxation* on their holiday have high hedonism and power. Interestingly, preference of *individual* holiday has negative correlation with hedonism.

Additionally, correlations between types of destinations and forms of holiday were tested. Correlation coefficients range from $r = 0.184$ to $r = 0.343$ ($p < 0.05$). *Seaside* is correlated with traveling abroad, for longer period of time and active participation. *Mountains* correlate with abroad and local traveling, for longer period of time and individual traveling. *City* is connected with longer traveling, in both large groups and individually and requires active participation on the holiday. *Spa* is correlated to traveling abroad and local, for longer period of time, individually. Visiting *villages* is correlated with the local traveling, individually with longer stays. Holiday on *river* is usually longer, in large groups and individually, with active participation and relaxation. *Lakes* are correlated with traveling abroad, longer holiday, both large groups' and individual travel and active participation.

Finally, average preference values and standard deviations, for each type of destination and form of holiday, were calculated. Most preferred type of destination is the seaside and least preferred is spa. Highest variations in responses were for city destination. Tourism abroad has the highest average of preference values while individual tourism has the lowest. Individual tourism has also the highest variation in responses.

CONCLUSION AND IMPLICATIONS

The goal of this research was to examine the relationship between individual values and holiday preferences. Both, types of destination and forms of holiday, are indirectly connected to holiday activities. Tourists expect to engage in certain activities depending on the type of destination (swimming on the seaside, skiing on the mountains, etc.) and depending on the form of holiday (short stay requires activities that are not time consuming, traveling abroad includes cultural exchange activities, etc.). Results indicate that there is a meaningful relationship between these two constructs.

Results of this study contribute to a better understanding of the tourism market and experts could use them in developing and improving marketing strategies for each type of destination and form of holiday. People who prefer seaside for their holiday are focused on personal success and stability. These tourists are more rigid and prefer to travel to familiar, secure destinations and they are focused on themselves more than on other people. Most of the tourists from Serbia nowadays travel to abroad seaside (such as Greece, Turkey, and Montenegro), since Serbia is a landlocked country. Many tourists go to the same seaside destination every year which is in accordance with the security value.

Mountain tourists are invested in others' well-being. They are helpful, loyal, and forgiving to others and believe that all people are equal. They also believe that nature and local community should be protected and preserved. Tourists from Serbia visit both local and abroad mountains and they prefer to go alone. So mountains attract strong individuals with love for nature and appreciation of diversity between people.

City tourists like freedom of thought and action but are also focused on self-interest. They need variety and stimulation from the surrounding and city seems to fulfill this need. They also seek prestige and social status which is apparently gained when visiting cities. Serbian tourists visit cities on their own or with large groups and they like active holiday which is in accordance with stimulation value domain.

Villages, on the other hand, visit people who value benevolence, universalism, and tradition. These are values that describe people who are concerned for others but rigid and dislike change and novelty. They need close friendly contact with people and local, traditional holidays. Villages seem to satisfy these needs. Rivers and lakes as destinations are correlated with the largest number of values.

Lakes have similar relationship with values as rivers but without correlations with values stimulation and tradition. This means that lake tourism attracts people with less rigid opinions, that don't need that much excitement but still require active participation in a certain amount. Visiting spas is not correlated significantly to any measured values. Spa tourism in Serbia is highly undeveloped and is still considered more a form of medical treatment for elderly than relaxation.

Traveling abroad highly attracts wide variety of people. It was something that was uncommon for a long period of time in Serbia, because of the sanctions and strict visa regime. Today, it is much easier to travel abroad because Serbia has an EU candidate status and no visas for most of the EU countries. People who travel abroad value other people and are tolerant. They also seek adventure and novelty and social acknowledgment of others.

Those who travel local also value other people and their opinions, but they are more rigid and love their country and customs. Longer, active holidays are for social people who prefer independent thought and creativity, who look for experience and strive for success.

Short holidays seem to be attractive for selfless people. People who enjoy life's pleasures and seek stimulation will travel with lots of people. Relaxing holiday draws people who need enjoyment in life and who like to feel powerful. Curiously, people who prefer to go on holiday on their own have negative relationship with hedonism. Those might be people who like to postpone their pleasures in life in order to achieve something in life. However, there were no significant correlations with achievement or self-direction. There is low positive correlation with spirituality, which might be significant with a larger and more diverse sample.

It is interesting to note that conformity has no significant correlations with any holiday preferences; it was only marginally positively correlated with local tourism. Every holiday is a time to let go, to enjoy, forget about the pressure for awhile. Self-restraint because of social norms seems to be relinquished when on holiday.

As every study, this has several limitations. One limitation is that for this research, only students were included in the sample. For more reliable results, different age and occupation groups should be included. Second limitation is that correlation coefficients were rather low but nevertheless significant. With larger, more diverse sample, this limitation should be overcome. This research should be extended to different cultures, to explore whether this relationship between values and holiday preferences is invariant. Also, possible moderators and mediators of this relationship should be explored (socio-demographic characteristics, previous experience with destinations, and forms of holiday).

ACKNOWLEDGMENT

This chapter received support from the Ministry of Education, Science and Technological Development, Republic of Serbia (Grant Number: 176020). Research that is presented here is a part of the doctoral research of Tamara Jovanovic.

REFERENCES

Backman, S. J., & Crompton, J. L. (1990). Differentiating between active and passive discontinuers of two leisure activities. *Journal of Leisure Research, 22*, 197–212.

Beatty, S. E., Kahle, L. R., & Homer, P. M. (1991). Personal values and gift giving behaviors: A study across cultures. *Journal of Business Research, 22,* 149–157.

Beatty, S. E., Kahle, L. R., Homer, P. M., & Mirsa, S. (1985). Alternative measurement approaches to consumer values: The list of values and the Rokeach value survey. *Psychology and Marketing, 3,* 181–200.

Crick-Furman, D., & Prentice, R. (2000). Modeling tourists' multiple values. *Annals of Tourism Research, 27*(1), 69–92.

Jackson, G. (1973). A preliminary bicultural study of value orientations and leisure attitudes. *Journal of Leisure Research, 5,* 10–22.

Jago, L. K. (1997). *Special events and tourism behaviour: A conceptualisation and an empirical analysis from a values perspective.* Ph.D. thesis, Victoria University.

Jovanovic, T., Majstorovic, N., Dinic, B., & Armenski, T. (2012, June 21–22). Applicability of Brand Personality Scale on travel destinations. Paper presented at the international conference on Destination Branding, Heritage and Authenticity – 1st EJTHR international conference, University of Santiago de Compostela, Santiago de Compostela.

Madrigal, R., & Kahle, L. R. (1994). Predicting vacation activity preferences on the basis of value-system segmentation. *Journal of Travel Research, 32*(3), 22–28.

McCleary, K. W., & Choi, B. M. (1999). Personal values as a base for segmenting international markets. *Tourism Analysis, 4*(1), 1–17.

Morrison, A. M., Hsieh, S., & O'Leary, J. T. (1994). Segmenting the Australian domestic travel market by holiday activity participation. *Journal of Tourism Studies, 5*(1), 39–56.

Muller, T. (1991). Using personal values to define segments in an international tourism market. *International Marketing Review, 8,* 57–70.

Pitts, R. E., & Woodside, A. G. (1986). Personal values and travel decisions. *Journal of Travel Research, 25,* 20–22.

Schwartz, S. H. (1992). Universals in the content and structure of values: Theoretical advances and empirical tests in 20 countries. In M. Zanna (Ed.), *Advances in Experimental Social Psychology* (pp. 1–65). Orlando, FL: Academic.

Schwartz, S. H. (1994). Are there universal aspects in the content and structure of values? *Journal of Social Issues, 50,* 19–45.

Schwartz, S. H., & Bilsky, W. (1987). Toward a psychological structure of human values. *Journal of Personality and Social Psychology, 53,* 550–562.

Schwartz, S. H., & Sagiv, L. (1995). Identifying culture-specifics in the content and structure of values. *Journal of Cross-Cultural Psychology, 26*(1), 92–116.

PARENTHOOD AND HOLIDAY DECISIONS: A GROUNDED THEORY APPROACH

Lidija Lalicic and Suzan Becks

ABSTRACT

This chapter investigates how holiday decisions for couples change when they become parents. By the use of a qualitative-explorative research approach (grounded theory method), 10 in-depth interviews were done with Dutch parents-to-be expecting their first child. The results show that emotional response ranks high in terms of the occurred changes, which originate from a set of interrelated consequences. A strong link with a deep fundamental basis rooted in daily life values can be made. Such roots oblige the tourism industry to consider product differentiation to serve this segment better and to capture a competitive position in the dynamic tourism industry.

Keywords: Consumer behavior; (holiday) decision-making process; life cycle stages

Tourists' Behaviors and Evaluations
Advances in Culture, Tourism and Hospitality Research, Volume 9, 59–64
Copyright © 2014 by Emerald Group Publishing Limited
All rights of reproduction in any form reserved
ISSN: 1871-3173/doi:10.1108/S1871-317320140000009006

INTRODUCTION

A comprehensible understanding of the interrelationships and densities of different variables in the holiday decision-making process is necessary as different authors argue (Kozak & Decrop, 2009; Sirakaya & Woodside, 2005; Smallman & Moore, 2010). The fact that tourists decide consciously as well as unconsciously about their holiday plan (Sirakaya & Woodside, 2005) and the strong influence of situational and social variables on this decision-making process (Payne, Bettman, Coupey, & Johnson, 1992) creates a difficult task to measure and understand this process. This study tries to approach these challenges of getting closer in unfolding the complexity of the holiday decision-making process. A person's position or transition in his or her life cycle is perceived as a major determinant of the holiday decision (Decrop, 2006). The aim of this study is to understand the factors that can explain how parenthood affects the decision-making process regarding a holiday and most importantly, the reasoning behind this.

THEORETICAL CONSIDERATIONS

The domain of holiday decision-making has been covered by a diversity of research. Tourists' decision-making processes involve many sub-decisions which occur continuously from prior to deciding "where to go" through to "what are we going to do now we are here" and beyond (Smallman & Moore, 2010). Motivations and emotional responses have been discussed as factors deriving changes. Constrains like time and emotional responses are key factors causing the meaning of attributes when children are involved (Kang, Hsu, & Wolfe, 2003; Nickerson & Jurowski, 2001; Ricci & del Missier, 2004; Thornton & Williams, 1997). Children also influence their parents by their expressive role and their demands during the holiday (Ricci & del Missier, 2004; Voigt & Laing, 2010). The link of understanding of why these values are interrelated, as well as influencing the decision-making process, remains unclear.

METHOD

Research has been struggling to take family dynamics in holiday decision-making into account (Carr, 2011). Different authors (Blichfeldt & Kessler,

2009; Smallman & Moore, 2010) argue that due to previous methodological choices, explanations about how and why factors within the decision-making process are interrelated, are limited. Therefore this study has taken a qualitative-explorative research approach by the use of the grounded theory. The data generation is built upon 10 in-depth interviews with Dutch parents-to-be expecting their first child, gathered between March and May 2011, by using snowball sampling. The couples got three topics to discuss: (1) overall holiday and travel activities, (2) general expectations and reasons, and (3) future holiday plans and expected influence due to their baby. Due to constant comparison in-between the interviews, it was also possible to reflect the emerging themes and changes to concepts and categories, which also assured the internal validity and a certain degree of inter-rater reliability, with independent two coders. Through the use of the consequences matrix (Fig. 1) and paradigm matrix (Fig. 2), visualization of dimensions, concepts, and categories were obtained and results could be confirmed.

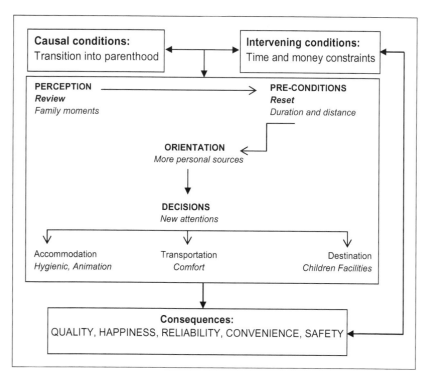

Fig. 1. Transition of the Decision-Making Process Due to Parenthood.

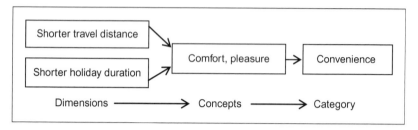

Fig. 2.   Development of Concept and Categories.

FINDINGS

This study shows that key decisions are mainly considered as a rational process and are deliberated quite intensely as argued by previous research. In particular, the concept of the "feeling-good" decisions by Decrop (2006) fits here. This study confirms variables such as destination, period, and duration being far less stable, as Decrop (2006) argues. The interviews exposed that changes occur in the decision-making process due to diverse restrictions such as money, time, children, and concerns. In addition, emotions rank high in terms of change and originate from a set of interrelated consequences known as quality, happiness, reliability, safety, and convenience. Obradors' (2012) supports the argument that family package holidays are saturated with ideas of intimacy, love, and togetherness. A holiday should stimulate feelings or emotional states in a tourist (Bansal & Eislet, 2003). However fundamental decisions within holidays are not affected by life cycle stages, for example, motivations such as "being away from home."

CONCLUSION AND IMPLICATIONS

This study shows that homogenous behavior among tourists entering parenthood is reflected in the determination of the weights they put on different aspects when considering decision changes due to entrance into parenthood. A link to Holbrook and Hirschman's (1982) argument can be made, that a holiday is one of those phenomena that include various lively activities, pleasures, and emotional responses. This study shows that emotions rank high in terms of change when transferring into the life cycle stage of parenthood. The interviews revealed that the emotional responses originate from a set of interrelated consequences known as quality, happiness, reliability, safety, and convenience. Additionally, this study shows that family holidays are important for reproduction of domesticity, as Obrador (2012) also claims. In this position, the holiday has been perceived as a part of daily life and should create a certain degree of added value which refers to a deeper fundamental basis. This value remains, however, stable along the continuum of Family-Life Cycle (FCL) stages and linked holiday decisions (Fodness, 1994). Therefore, it can be argued that this study contributed to the decision-making literature by going beyond the scope of family holidays.

The holiday has been perceived as a part of daily life and should create a certain degree of added value which refers to a deeper fundamental basis. Therefore, it can be argued that this study contributed to the decision-making literature by going beyond the scope of family holidays. For the tourism industry, there is a need to introduce new and/or added components that can create feelings parents require for the overall holiday experience. The shift to parenthood mainly relies on consequences that can be served by different characteristics in a holiday package, like children animation and accommodation with high hygienic standards. To surmount the limitations of this study, observational method would have to be employed. The collection of information relating to decision-making can only evoke faults if the research would take place after the couples transform into parents-to-be though a setting of a longitudinal study. In addition, generalization should be carefully taken into account in terms of cultural backgrounds, which can devise changes as well.

REFERENCES

Bansal, H., & Eislet, H. A. (2003). Exploratory research of tourist motivations and planning. *Tourism Management, 25,* 387–396.
Blichfeldt, B. S., & Kessler, I. (2009). Interpretive consumer research, under covering "whys" underlying tourist behaviour. In M. Kozak & A. Decrop (Eds.), *Handbook of tourist behaviour, theory & practice* (pp. 3–15). New York, NY: Routledge.
Carr, N. (2011). *Children's and families holidays experiences.* London: Taylor & Francis.
Decrop, A. (2006). *Vacation decision making.* Oxon: CABI.
Fodness, D. (1994). Measuring tourist motivation. *Annals of Tourism Research, 21*(3), 555–581.
Holbrook, M. B., & Hirschman, C. E. (1982). The experiential aspects of consumption, consumer fantasies and fun. *The Journal of Consumer Research, 9*(2), 132–140.
Kang, S. K., Hsu, C. H. C., & Wolfe, K. (2003). Family traveller segmentation by vacation decision-making patterns. *Journal of Hospitality and Tourism Research, 27*(4), 458–469.

Kozak, M., & Decrop, A. (Eds.). (2009). *Handbook of tourist behavior: Theory & practice*. London: Routledge.

Obrador, P. (2012). The place of the family in tourism research: Domesticity and thick sociality by the pool. *Annals of Tourism Research, 39*(1), 401−420.

Payne, J. W., Bettman, J. R., Coupey, E., & Johnson, E. J. (1992). A constructive process view of decision making: Multiple strategies in judgment and choice. *Acta Psychologica, 80*(1), 107–141.

Ricci, F., & Del Missier F. (2004). Supporting travel decision making through personalized recommendation. In K. Clare-Marie, B. Jan, & K. John (Eds.), *Designing personalized user experiences for e-Commerce* (pp. 221–251). Dordrecht: Kluwer Academic Publisher.

Sirakaya, E., & Woodside, A. G. (2005). Building and testing theories of decision making by travellers. *Tourism Management, 26*(6), 815–832.

Smallman, C., & Moore, K. (2010). Process studies of tourists decision-making. *Annals of Tourism Research, 37*(2), 397–422.

Thornton, P. R., & Williams, A. M. (1997). Tourist group holiday decision making and behaviour: The influence of children. *Tourism Management, 18*(5), 287−297.

Voigt, C., & Laing, J. H. (2010). Journey into parenthood: Commodification of reproduction as a new tourism nice market. *Journal of Travel & Tourism Marketing, 27*(3), 252−268.

IT CAN'T HAPPEN TO ME: TRAVEL RISK PERCEPTIONS

Brent W. Ritchie, P. Monica Chien and
Bernadette M. Watson

ABSTRACT

Although the significance of travel risks is well documented, the process through which people assess their vulnerability and ultimately take on preventive measures needs clarification. Motivated by concern with traveler's underestimation of risks, this chapter provides a crucial next step by introducing new theory to explain how people calibrate travel risks. The conceptual model incorporates constructs from motivational theories, cognitive appraisal, and emotionality. Future studies adopting this model will broaden the nature and scope of research on travel risk while helping government and industry to increase the reach and relevance of travel health and safety messages.

Keywords: Risk perception; risk prevention; travel health; marketing communication; tourist behavior

Tourists' Behaviors and Evaluations
Advances in Culture, Tourism and Hospitality Research, Volume 9, 65–73
Copyright © 2014 by Emerald Group Publishing Limited
All rights of reproduction in any form reserved
ISSN: 1871-3173/doi:10.1108/S1871-317320140000009008

INTRODUCTION

Tourist destinations are often located in hazard prone locations (Ritchie, 2008). Tourists tend to be at higher levels of exposure to a range of health and safety hazards during a vacation than local residents due to lack of familiarity or unwillingness to exercise caution (McInnes, Williamson, & Morrison, 2002). Around 50% of travelers will report some kind of illness or injury when traveling overseas (Behrens, 1997). Problems include diseases transmitted through food and water, infectious diseases, and accidents caused by careless behaviors, while attending mass gatherings may further amplify viral exchange. For example, infectious disease caused the death of 2.4% of Australians who died while traveling overseas (Schemierer & Jackson, 2006). Yet, 28% of Australians traveled overseas without travel insurance, while 60% of travelers did not get vaccinated prior to international travel (DFAT, 2012). Clearly, current public campaigns intending to increase one's susceptibility to travel associated risks have been ineffective to influence travelers' precautionary behavior. These statistics highlight the size of the problem.

THEORETICAL CONSIDERATIONS

Because the degree to which a traveler believes that he or she is at risk affects decisions to engage in preventive behaviors, an understanding of the process by which travelers construct risk perceptions is a vital first step. This chapter builds a conceptual framework that identifies a number of antecedents of travel risk perception and represents an initial attempt to understand travel risk prevention behavior from a consumercentric perspective. As a foundation for future research, we develop key propositions using theories from social psychology and propose methods for empirical studies.

Travel risk perception is defined as the negatively valenced likelihood assessment that an unfavorable event will occur over a specified time period (Menon, Raghubir, & Agrawal, 2008). This chapter focuses on physical risks that encompass health and safety hazards as (1) physical risks are commonplace and, if encountered, are likely to have psychological, financial, and even social implications to the traveler as well as the country's healthcare system; and (2) many risks can be prevented or their impact can be minimized through precautionary behaviors, such as being immunized or covered by insurance.

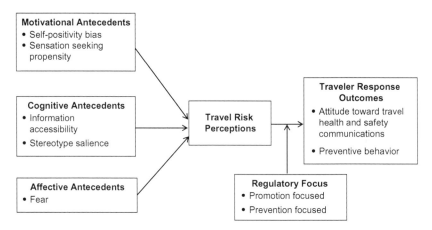

Fig. 1. Conceptual Model of Travel Risk Perception.

Extant research on travel risks mainly focuses on risk generators at the destination level or variables idiosyncratic to a specific trip (e.g., Jonas, Mansfeld, Paz, & Potasman, 2010), risk classification (e.g., Roehl & Fesenmaier, 1992) or examine issues related to travelers' socio-demographic characteristics (e.g., Seabra et al., 2012), thus only measure a small number of constructs. The broader psychological mechanisms that contribute to travelers' risk perceptions have been overlooked in past studies.

To address this gap, the proposed conceptual model combines perspectives from Protection Motivation Theory (PMT: Rogers, 1983) and the health risk perceptions model (Menon et al., 2008) with literature on travel risk, thus providing a broader road-map for studying the psychology of travel risk perception. The central theory is that travelers' risk estimates and intention to engage in preventive behaviors is a function of innate appraisal processes. A novel feature of the model is the identification of a multilevel set of psychological constructs proposed to influence the formation of travel risk perception. These constructs are divided into three antecedent categories: motivational, cognitive, and affective (Fig. 1).

PROPOSITIONS AND RATIONALE

Motivational Antecedents

The first motivational antecedent, self-positivity bias, refers to people's tendency to believe that bad things are less likely to happen to them than to the average person (Raghubir & Menon, 1998). It is a motivational bias that self is more invulnerable than others and thus impervious to the threats or hazards – an "It cannot happen to me" syndrome (Weinstein, 1980). Self-positivity effect may be due to an overall desire to feel happy and to maintain or enhance self-esteem (Raghubir & Menon, 1998). Such an idea implies not only a hopeful outlook on life, but an error in judgment that can be labeled unrealistic optimism (Weinstein, 1980). Thus, if self-positivity bias is in operation, people would perceive themselves as being less risk-prone than others in the same risk group (e.g., other travelers) and are unrealistically optimistic about their chances of experiencing negative events (Menon et al., 2008). Similarly, travelers would assume that they are less at risk than others and may tune out preventative messaged directed to them, diminishing the effectiveness of public education campaigns.

Proposition 1. Travelers with high self-positivity bias perceive lower likelihood of experiencing negative events compared to travelers with low self-positivity bias.

Sensation-seeking propensity (SSP) is another motivational factor that intertwines with perception of risk. Sensation-seeking is a personality trait in which individuals are considered to vary in their ability to tolerate sensations of all types (Pizam, Jeong, Reichel, van Boemmel, & Lusson, 2004). People with the desire for novelty and intense sensory stimulation show their willingness to take risks for the sake of such experience. Therefore, sensation-seeking is considered to be a predisposition which may be expressed in a number of ways, such as increased preferences for intense, novel, and high-risk recreational activities, rather than structured and repetitive low-risk activities (Galloway & Lopez, 1999; Pizam et al., 2004).

Proposition 2. Travelers with high SSP perceive lower likelihood of experiencing negative events compared to travelers with low SSP.

Cognitive Antecedents

Two cognitive factors may underpin travelers' estimation of risks: information accessibility and stereotype salience. Travel risk perception should be a function of the number and type of risk experiences that are accessible in memory (Menon et al., 2008). The greater the number of experiences that can be accessed, the higher should be the perception of one's own risk as people should sum every single risk experience retrieved. Raghubir and Menon (1998) showed that when AIDS-related behaviors were easier to retrieve from memory, people reported a higher risk of AIDS than when it was less accessible in memory. Information accessibility can be affected by the frequency and recency of activation of information in memory (Feldman & Lynch, 1988). Thus, travelers' risk perceptions can be a reflection of past risk-related experiences insofar as they occur regularly and recently. The more frequent and recent that experience is, the higher the information accessibility, and the more easily information comes to mind (Feldman & Lynch, 1988). When information comes to mind easily, people are more confident about the probability of an event occurring (Raghubir & Menon, 1998). Prior experience with a threatening event increases sensitivity to risks because it makes risks easier to imagine.

Proposition 3. Travelers who can easily access risk-related information from memory perceive higher likelihood of experiencing negative events compared to travelers who cannot easily access risk-related information from memory.

Stereotype salience refers to the extent to which people have a stereotyped conception of the kind of person to whom negative events happen (Heine & Lehman, 1995). It is the process of judging the probability that an individual fits into a particular category by examining the degree to which the individual displays salient features of category members (Thornton, Gibbons, & Gerrard, 2002). For many events, such as contracting AIDS or having a lung cancer, people may have a stereotyped conception of the kind of people to whom the event happens. Weinstein (1980) found that people reported greater relative invulnerability for negative events for which they could easily visualize the type of person to experience them. That is, people use the stereotype as the representativeness heuristic. If they do not see themselves as fitting the stereotype, they will conclude that the negative event will not happen to them. Such victim stereotypes serve an ego-defensive function and produce optimism for negative events as well as an exaggeration of risk immunity (Heine & Lehman, 1995). Intuitively, if travelers do not see themselves fitting the stereotypic victim, they are likely to conclude that the negative events will not happen to them and thus have lower risk perception.

Proposition 4. Travelers who hold a salient risk stereotype perceive lower likelihood of experiencing negative events compared to travelers who hold a vague risk stereotype.

Affective Antecedent

As emotion is hypothesized to trigger changes in cognition and action, a growing literature in psychology considers the interplay of affect and risk perceptions (Lench & Levine, 2005). For a traveler, the imminent trip may arouse varied emotions, such as fear and happiness. In particular, fear may be evoked by appraisal that the individual has little power or control over certain situations (e.g., contracting malaria), the outcome is uncertain, and a goal (e.g., a carefree holiday) may be threatened (Lench & Levine, 2005). Fear generates a feeling of uncertainty, primes pessimism, and leads fearful individuals to make risk-averse decisions (Lerner & Keltner, 2001). Consequently, fearful people should rate negative events as more likely to occur and will tune in to information that is relevant to the source of their fear.

Proposition 5. Travelers who experience high fear perceive higher likelihood of experiencing negative events compared to travelers who experience low fear.

Travel Risk Perception and Traveler Response Outcomes

At the heart of virtually all models of health behavior is an individual's perception of risk (e.g., Rogers, 1983). Common to these models is the hypothesis that perceived vulnerability is the major motivational force behind preventive behavior. Some studies have demonstrated a link between low-risk perceptions and low levels of precautionary behavior, while others have shown that raising perceptions of personal risk can effectively enhance subsequent precautionary behaviors (Thornton et al., 2002). Analogously, travelers who think they are at risk are likely to engage in precautionary behavior.

Proposition 6. Travelers who perceive lower likelihood of experiencing negative events will (a) will have a more negative attitude toward travel health and safety communications and (b) have lower intention to undertake preventive behavior, compared to travelers who perceive higher likelihood of experiencing negative events.

Regulatory Focus as a Moderator

Some researchers, however, question the hypothesized link between risk perception and preventive behavior (Thornton et al., 2002), suggesting that increasing risk perceptions may not always encourage people to seek out preventive actions, and high-risk perception may even turn away processing of preventive communication (Menon et al., 2008). Building on PMT (Rogers, 1983), the current model proposes that people will evaluate response efficacy of the advocated actions and identifies an individual's regulatory focus as a moderator of the effect of travel risk perception. Regulatory focus is a psychological mechanism that serves as a fundamental driver of attitudes and plays a motivating role in directing people's behaviors (Aaker & Lee, 2006). Prevention focused individuals regulate their attitudes and behaviors to ensure safety, responsibilities, and obligations. They are sensitive to the presence and absence of negative outcomes, thus they may be more responsive to messages that advocate careful actions and emphasize avoidance of potential losses (Aaker & Lee, 2006). In contrast, promotion-focused individuals regulate their attitudes and behaviors to attain growth and achievement. As they are sensitive to the presence and absence of positive outcomes, messages that emphasize achievement of potential gains will be more effective (Aaker & Lee, 2006). When travelers encounter health and safety messages that fit with their regulatory focus (i.e., regulatory fit), they experience heightened motivation and an "it-just-feels-right" sensation, which leads to more positive response outcomes.

Proposition 7. Individuals' regulatory focus moderates the effect of travel risk perception on traveler response outcomes.

In summary, our model differentiates from existing studies on travel risk perception in three aspects: (1) the integration of a broader sets of motivational, cognitive, and affective factors; (2) the inclusion of regulatory focus as a moderator of risk perception; (3) the consideration of both attitude toward travel health and safety communications and intention to engage in preventive behaviors as traveler response outcomes. Future studies can adopt a cross-sectional survey to empirically test the hypothesized relationships between travel risk perception, its antecedents, and impact on traveler response outcomes. Field experiments which manipulate the genres of travel health and safety messages can also be used to examine the regulatory fit assumption put forward by the conceptual model.

CONCLUSION AND IMPLICATIONS

This chapter explores how travelers' general predispositions toward risk manifest in their assessment of travel risks and response outcomes.

Through the development of an integrative theoretical model, this chapter uncovers innate psychological factors that underlie travel risk appraisal process, providing an important insights of traveler behavior to both researchers and practitioners. As the research integrates concepts from the domains of tourist behavior, social psychology, and marketing, it greatly expands the nature and scope of investigations on travel risk perception and management. Specifically, the model identifies an individual's regulatory focus as a moderating variable, a motivational instrument which has not been previously applied to understanding travelers' behavior. The mechanism provides an impetus to turn perception into action and explains why high-risk perception does not always lead to behavioral change.

This chapter provides auxiliary benefits for government and industry. For example, the overall number of Australian tourists seeking out consular services has grown significantly placing a considerable burden upon Department of Foreign Affairs and Trade (DFAT) consular services. The conceptual model could be used to address sources of risk perception and has implications on the design and development of risk communications.

The costs to travelers who encounter health and safety problems overseas are high. This chapter contributes to increased knowledge of traveler information processing and provides market intelligence to government bodies and industry. Realistic assessment of risk allows the individual to make better informed travel decisions, which may lower the chances of negative events ruining holiday plans and effectively reduce the burden on government operations and management.

REFERENCES

Aaker, J. L., & Lee, A. Y. (2006). Understanding regulatory fit. *Journal of Marketing Research, 43*(1), 15−19.

Behrens, R. (1997). Important issues influencing the health of travellers. In S. Clift & P. Grabowski (Eds.), *Tourism and health: Risks, research and responses* (pp. 38−47). London: Pinter.

DFAT. (2012). *Department of foreign affairs and trade annual report 2011−2012.* Commonwealth Government of Australia, Canberra.

Feldman, J. M., & Lynch, J. G. (1988). Self-generated validity and other effects of measurement on belief, attitude, intention, and behavior. *Journal of Applied Psychology, 73*(3), 421−435.

Galloway, G., & Lopez, K. (1999). Sensation seeking and attitudes to aspects of national parks: A preliminary empirical investigation. *Tourism Management, 20*(6), 665−671.

Heine, S. J., & Lehman, D. R. (1995). Cultural variation in unrealistic optimism: Does the west feel more vulnerable than the east? *Journal of Personality and Social Psychology, 68*(4), 595–607.

Jonas, A., Mansfeld, Y., Paz, S., & Potasman, I. (2010). Determinants of health risk perception among low-risk-taking tourists traveling to developing countries. *Journal of Travel Research, 50*(1), 87–99.

Lench, H. C., & Levine, L. J. (2005). Effects of fear on risk and control judgements and memory: Implications for health promotion messages. *Cognition and Emotion, 19*(7), 1049–1069.

Lerner, J. S., & Keltner, D. (2001). Fear, anger, and risk. *Journal of Personality and Social Psychology, 81*(1), 146–159.

McInnes, R., Williamson, L. M., & Morrison, A. (2002). Unintentional injury during foreign travel: A review. *Journal of Travel Medicine, 9*(6), 297–307.

Menon, G., Raghubir, P., & Agrawal, N. (2008). Health risk perceptions and consumer psychology. In C. P. Haugtvedt, P. M. Herr, & F. R. Kardes (Eds.), *Handbook of consumer psychology* (pp. 981–1010). New York, NY: Laurence Erlbaum.

Pizam, A., Jeong, G. H., Reichel, A., van Boemmel, H., & Lusson, J. M. (2004). The relationship between risk-taking, sensation-seeking, and the tourist behavior of young adults: A cross-cultural study. *Journal of Travel Research, 42*(3), 251–260.

Raghubir, P., & Menon, G. (1998). AIDS and me, never the twain shall meet: The effects of information accessibility on judgments of risk and advertising effectiveness. *Journal of Consumer Research, 25*(1), 52–63.

Ritchie, B. W. (2008). Tourism disaster planning and management: From response and recovery to reduction and readiness. *Current Issues in Tourism, 11*(4), 315–348.

Roehl, W. S., & Fesenmaier, D. R. (1992). Risk perceptions and pleasure travel: An exploratory analysis. *Journal of Travel Research, 30*(4), 17–26.

Rogers, R. W. (1983). Cognitive and physiological processes in fear appeals and attitude change: A revised theory of protection motivation. In J. Cacioppo & R. Petty (Eds.), *Social psychophysiology* (pp. 153–176). New York, NY: Guilford Press.

Schemierer, C., & Jackson, M. (2006). Local health impacts of tourism. In J. Wilks, D. Pendergast, & P. Leggat (Eds.), *Tourism in turbulent times: Towards safe experiences for visitors* (pp. 63–75). Oxford: Elsevier.

Seabra, C., Dolnicar, S., Abrantes, J. L., & Kastenholz, E. (2012). Heterogeneity in risk and safety perceptions of international tourists. *Tourism Management, 36*, 502–510.

Thornton, B., Gibbons, F. X., & Gerrard, M. (2002). Risk perception and prototype perception: Independent processes predicting risk behavior. *Personality and Social Psychology Bulletin, 28*(7), 986–999.

Weinstein, N. D. (1980). Unrealistic optimism about future life events. *Journal of Personality and Social Psychology, 39*(5), 806–820.

ADOPTION OF INFORMATION AND COMMUNICATIONS TECHNOLOGY (ICT) BY IN-TRIP LEISURE TOURISTS

Mareba M. Scott and Andrew J. Frew

ABSTRACT

This chapter examines the factors influencing actual in-trip information and communications technology usage by leisure tourists and the potential of adopted technologies to support sustainable tourism. Thirty semi-structured interviews were conducted in the city of Edinburgh. A thematic analysis of the data revealed that consistent with the literature, perceived ease of use, perceived usefulness, and social influence affected usage while in-trip. Tourists' level of personal innovativeness also moderated smartphone ownership and actual usage while in the destination. Location-based services and social media proved to be the applications which enjoyed the most usage and the greatest opportunities to promote sustainability.

Keywords: ICT; sustainable tourism

Tourists' Behaviors and Evaluations
Advances in Culture, Tourism and Hospitality Research, Volume 9, 75–84
Copyright © 2014 by Emerald Group Publishing Limited
All rights of reproduction in any form reserved
ISSN: 1871-3173/doi:10.1108/S1871-317320140000009009

INTRODUCTION

Technology plays a role in all phases of the holiday experience – from the point of dreaming and researching, to the purchase, during the trip, and post-trip. Tourism as we know it today has made significant strides because of technology, and for many destinations it is a source of their competitive advantage (Buhalis & O'Connor, 2005). In some contexts, technology for tourists reduces perceived purchasing risk, provides competitive prices, facilitates the purchasing process, offers opportunities for self-packaging, and allows the co-creation of experiences during and after the trip (Neuhofer, Buhalis, & Ladkin, 2012). Technology therefore adds value to tourists' experiences during all phases of travel.

Consumer behavior during the planning phase, that is, pre-trip has been extensively researched (e.g., Fodness & Murray, 1998; Sirakaya & Woodside, 2005; Woodside, Krauss, Caldwell, & Chebat, 2007); however, how technology mediates the in-trip tourism experience receives scant attention in the relevant literature. Very limited knowledge about in-trip tourists' actual use of information and communications technology (ICT) and sustainable tourism is available. Given the ubiquitous nature of technology in travel and tourism, substantial opportunities exist to use technology in ways that improve the tourist experience; consumption patterns; and assist in the internalization of sustainability principles. The application of ICT for sustainable tourism development and actual in-trip usage are under-researched areas. This chapter aims to examine the factors influencing actual in-trip ICT usage by leisure tourists and the extent to which adopted technologies could support sustainable tourism.

THEORETICAL CONSIDERATIONS

Despite the contentious nature of defining sustainable tourism, many scholars do agree that it should be the goal of tourism destinations to develop in a manner where the deleterious effects of tourism are minimized and the positive benefits are maximized. Sustainable tourism has been defined as tourism that considers current and future economic, social, cultural, and environmental impacts, while fulfilling the needs of visitors, the industry, and the host communities. All tourism should thrive to develop sustainably, whether as an emerging or mass tourism destination. The United Nations Environmental Programme and World Tourism Organization (2005) outlined 12 aims of sustainable tourism: economic viability, local prosperity, employment quality, social equity, visitor fulfillment, local control, community wellbeing, cultural richness, physical integrity, biological diversity, resource efficiency, and environmental purity. These aims provide a useful frame of reference to illustrate how in-trip ICTs can be used to support sustainable tourism.

While the acceptance of the principles of sustainable tourism has grown, natural resources, many of which are consumed by tourists' activities are increasingly under threat. Sharpley (2009, p. 68) notes, "Despite surveys which suggest that tourists are increasingly aware of the impacts of their activities and hence, claim they adapt their behavior accordingly, there is little empirical evidence of the adoption of such behavior in practice." Lamsfus, Xiang, Alzua-Sorzabal, and Martin (2013) suggest that today's mobile technologies have the ability to change tourists' behavioral patterns. Thus, technology can serve as an integrating tool to support the modification of consumer behavior and by extension get tourists to participate in more sustainable tourism activities.

Technology acceptance receives much attention in the organizational context with the technology acceptance model (TAM) (Davis, 1989), an extended version referred to as TAM2 (Venkatesh & Davis, 2000), and the unified theory of acceptance and use of technology (UTAUT) (Venkatesh, Morris, Davis, & Davis, 2003) frequently cited. Initial work by Davis (1989) focuses on perceived usefulness (PU) and perceived ease of use (PEOU), which were theorized to be fundamental antecedents of system use. In the UTAUT, Venkatesh et al. (2003) theorize that four constructs determine user acceptance and usage behavior: performance expectancy, effort expectancy, social influence, and facilitating conditions. Venkatesh et al. (2003) also postulate that age, gender, experience, and voluntariness would have moderating effects on behavioral intentions, which ultimately predicts use behavior.

Among the criticisms leveled against the TAMs has been the focus on intention rather than actual use. Baron, Patterson, and Harris (2006) argue that measurement of the variables in TAM and extensions of the TAM have been too reliant on simplistic items of measurement. They note that previous measurements ignore the technology paradoxes (Mick & Fournier, 1998), and advocate that the development of theory associated with perceived enjoyment, PU, and PEOU should not be confined by the existing quantitative models of technology, but draw more on the theory from studies of consumer practices (Baron et al., 2006).

Anckar and D'Incau (2002) suggest that for consumers on the move, time critical arrangements, spontaneous needs, entertainment needs, efficiency ambitions, and mobile situations are important value creating elements.

Eriksson and Strandvik (2009) used the TAM and UTAUT to identify possible determinants of intended or actual use of mobile tourism services. These antecedents include value, ease of use, risk, social influence, and tourist characteristics (which include demographic variables (gender, age), experience of mobile services, travel experience, destination experience, type of travel, personal innovativeness, and user device readiness). A qualitative approach with tourists actively engaged in ICT use could serve to extend the knowledge about use behavior in the consumer domain.

METHOD

This chapter represents phase two of a mixed method research approach where the qualitative component constituted the dominant element of the investigation. Phase one assisted in the development of the semi-structured interview protocol. The adopted qualitative approach served to answer the research question: What factors will influence tourist using/not using ICT tools or applications that could make tourism at their destination more sustainable?

The main unit of analysis was domestic and international in-trip tourists visiting the city of Edinburgh. Thirty semi-structured interviews were conducted at six studies sites – The National Gallery Complex, St. Giles Cathedral, National Museum of Scotland, Edinburgh Castle, Edinburgh Zoo, and Princes Gardens. The researcher used thematic analysis to iden-tify themes and key theoretical constructs from the transcribed interviews. Themes were identified based on categories of data established a priori as well as those emerging from the data.

FINDINGS

Apart from the manifest themes that were developed a priori, at the latent level, several emergent themes gave an insight into use and non-use of ICT tools/applications by the in-trip leisure tourists. In-trip technologies were later analyzed relative to their ability to support sustainable tourism.

SOCIAL CONNECTION

Social connection was an emergent theme and defined as actions displayed by tourists to maintain (or minimize) contact with family, relatives, or friends. The theme underlying the desire of those with standard mobile phones to purchase a smartphone was the maintenance of "social connections." This is exemplified in the following excerpts by interviewees Jave and Stephan:

> ... I'm doing travelling and I wanted to stay connected with family back ... just to be connected. (Jave)

> No, I just have a very old cell phone and maybe this time is the first time that I think that I have to buy one because I am very used to when I'm travelling to look for an Internet point ... maybe after this trip I will need ... I will think to buy also some new technology about my cell phone. To be connected also. (Stephan)

Clear differences occur between standard mobile users and smartphone users in how social connectedness was maximized or minimized based on the affiliative needs of the individual. Facebook was popular for maintaining social connections however, the importance, purpose, and the type of social media accessed varied across interviewees. Stephan, for example, used Couchsurfing for creating new social connections while others used social media for checking reviews (e.g., TripAdvisor), contacting family (e.g., via Whatsapp and Facebook), or liaising with friends about what to do or where to go.

According to Baron and Harris (2010, p. 50), the benefits from C2C interactions are deeper than the C2B relationship and as such social media provides an opportunity for "social interaction, to express concern for others, and to enhance self-worth." The in-trip destination experience is enriched by the tourist's ability to virtually engage with other consumers (e.g., TripAdvisor), friends and relatives (e.g., via Facebook), and tourism suppliers (via location-based services such as Yelp). Couchsurfing as a form of social media represents a unique type of co-creation between the visitor and locals which can enhance the authenticity of the destination experience. Therefore, location-based services and social media contribute directly to the destinations sustainability as it enhances visitor fulfillment, economic viability, local prosperity, cultural richness, and community wellbeing.

PERSONAL INNOVATIVENESS

Interviewees were asked to describe their technological expertise and then asked how quickly they acquire new technology relative to their friends or colleagues. The responses to these questions provided insights about an individual's level of personal innovativeness (PI) – willingness to try out or

embrace new technology. Interviewees that demonstrated a high level of
PI were smartphone owners and used their smartphone while in-trip.
Some had two devices (a smartphone and a tablet) and one interviewee
(Brian) even had three devices – a smartphone, a tablet, and a lap-top.
Interviewees with a high level of PI also had a high level of on-the-job tech-
nological use.

Interviewees with a low-level of PI generally did not own smartphones
and either relied on traditional sources of information (e.g., guide books)
or their traveling partner's smartphone for use in-trip for Internet searches,
weather forecast and maps, or GPS functions. Those interviewees who
were classified with low levels of PI were far more effusive in their views on
their unwillingness to embrace new technology. Some interviewees did not
demonstrate a general resistance to technology but were less enthusiastic
for some types of applications (e.g., Facebook); additionally some interviewees simultaneously expressed both positive and negative views of
technology–technology paradoxes (Mick & Fournier, 1998).

PEOU AND PU

Consistent with the literature, interviewees, in the main, indicated that
either PEOU or PU would be a main factor influencing technological use.
The following excerpts provide a sample of responses to the question on
factors influencing use:

> How easy it is to use. I mean can I quickly find what I need to find especially in terms
> of maps ..., and then can I share this information with friends .... (Brian)

> I think the ease-of-use .... (Chris)

> It would have to be something that I ... To be able to function ... it would have to be
> that vital .... (Louise)

SOCIAL INFLUENCE AND SOCIAL MEDIA

The desired level of social connectedness influenced not only in-trip technological usage but also the type of social media used. The types of social
media used in-trip by the leisure tourists and the use of some technological
tools and applications were influenced by the importance individuals

attached to different types of referent groups, for example, family or friends or other travelers. Social influence and the use of social media is not a unidirectional process; the co-creation process means that tourists also have the ability to influence the views of others while in-trip and post-trip through various types of applications. Renu recognized this collaborative process in his use of Instagram and Foursquare, and stressed how important recommendations were to the value-creation of the touristic experience.

A number of the interviewees had negative views about social media and demonstrated a desire to minimize social connections through this medium. Notably, such views were not limited to the standard mobile phone users but extended to the smartphone users as well.

PERCEIVED ENJOYMENT

A number of tourists made references to "checking-in" via social media while in-trip (e.g., Renu, Louise, Brian) and Renu mentioned that he was a "Mayor" in a number of places. The use of social media in such instances was beyond the utilitarian function and provided an element of fun to users. Jens had brought along a large GPS to engage in geo-caching while in-trip and Miriam's use of her iPad while in-trip was solely to play a game. Renu also referred to the use of his iPad while in-trip to watch films while Janet emphasized the use of her iPad for entertainment, including playing games.

The use of maps and GPS functions contribute to visitor fulfillment and tended to be used across the board by smartphone users, irrespective of age. Apart from adding to PE and visitor fulfillment, social media and gaming can also support other sustainable tourism aims, such as cultural richness, physical integrity, resource efficiency, and environmental purity.

SUSTAINABLE TOURISM-TECHNOLOGY LINKAGE

One of the questions that leisure tourists were asked that provided insights into whether they perceived a link between sustainable tourism and technology was: What role do you think technology or a travel application can play in making a tourist destination more sustainable?

General questions about sustainable tourism demonstrated an environmental conception and only a few tourists had holistic perspectives about
sustainable tourism. As such, not everyone saw a linkage between sustainable tourism and technology and some interviewees openly said so, for
example, Anna said, "I don't see how it could be, I don't see how an app
can help the sustainability of anywhere," while a few others indicated that
they hadn't given it much thought (e.g., Susan and Jens). Some interviewees
immediately saw an environmental benefit by reducing the production of
paper-based brochures and maps and instead using travel applications or
digital interactive displays. Such limited views about sustainability should
come as no surprise given sustainable tourism's environmental roots
described in the literature.

CONCLUSION AND IMPLICATIONS

While all the in-trip tourists interviewed owned a standard mobile tele-
phone, they did not all have smartphones which meant that the destination
experience for some may have been less co-created. However, with reduced
cost, smartphone ownership is likely to increase in time, and usage will be
more widespread. The in-trip phase presents destination managers with
multiple opportunities for co-creating experiences (Neuhofer et al., 2012),
which enhances the visitors' satisfaction but can also support local prosperity, economic viability, cultural richness and community wellbeing.

Social media though unpopular with some tourists was well utilized by
younger visitors and as suggested by Miller, Rathouse, Scarles, Holmes,
and Tribe (2010) could be a powerful tool in bringing about behavioral
change. Connectedness, functionality, and experiences must be central to
the design of in-trip tourism applications and destinations need to find
creative ways and use multiple channels to not only promote in-trip applications but to embed sustainability into such products. Further research is
needed on the role of perceived enjoyment and mobile value elements and
its influence on PEOU and PU, in the tourism domain. Investigation is also
needed on how specific tourist traits moderate use behavior and how these
behaviors vary across tourism markets.

PI was not defined as a tourist trait by Baron et al. (2006), however;
based on this research and work of other theorists, PI is a trait that replaces
perceived behavioral control within a revised theoretical construct for the
consumer TAM, and as a predictive element of intention and ultimately

use. PI and mobile value elements are crucial to understanding technology adoption by in-trip tourists. Destination management organizations have the opportunity to respond in real-time and use technology to manage the visitor's experience. Activities designed to promote sustainability in the destination can be incentivized to build loyalty and encourage positive e-Word Of Mouth (e-WOM) and simultaneously gather marketing intelligence for the customization of strategies for the future.

REFERENCES

Anckar, B., & D'Incau, D. (2002). Value creation in mobile commerce: Findings from a consumer survey. *The Journal of Information Technology Theory and Application, 4*(1), 43–64.

Baron, S., & Harris, K. (2010). Toward an understanding of consumer perspectives on experiences. *Journal of Services Marketing, 24*(7), 518–531.

Baron, S., Patterson, S., & Harris, K. (2006). Beyond technology acceptance: Understanding consumer practice. *International Journal of Service Industry Management, 17*(2), 111–135.

Buhalis, D., & O'Connor, P. (2005). Information and communication technology revolutionizing tourism. *Tourism Recreation Research, 30*(3), 7–16.

Davis, F. D. (1989). Perceived usefulness, perceived ease of use, and user acceptance of information technology. *MIS Quarterly, 13*(3), 319–340.

Eriksson, N., & Strandvik, P. (2009). Possible determinants affecting the use of mobile tourism services. In J. Filipe & M. S. Obaidat (Eds.), *eBusiness and telecommunications* (pp. 61–73). Berlin Heidelberg: Springer-Verlag.

Fodness, D., & Murray, B. (1998). A typology of tourist information search strategies. *Journal of Travel Research, 37*, 108–119.

Lamsfus, C., Xiang, Z., Alzua-Sorzabal, A., & Martin, D. (2013). Conceptualizing context in an intelligent mobile environment in travel and tourism. In L. Cantoni & Z. Xiang (Eds.), *Information and communications technologies in tourism 2013* (pp. 1–11). Innsbruck, NY: Springer-Verlag.

Mick, D., & Fournier, S. (1998). Paradoxes of technology: Consumer cognizance, emotions, and coping strategies. *Journal of Consumer Research, 25*(2), 123–143.

Miller, G., Rathouse, K., Scarles, C., Holmes, K., & Tribe, J. (2010). Public understanding of sustainable tourism. *Annals of Tourism Research, 37*(3), 627–645.

Neuhofer, B., Buhalis, D., & Ladkin, A. (2012). Conceptualising technology enhanced experiences. *Journal of Destination Marketing & Management, 1*, 36–46.

Sharpley, R. (2009). *Tourism development and the environment: Beyond sustainability?* London: Earthscan.

Sirakaya, E., & Woodside, A. (2005). Building and testing theories of decision making by travellers. *Tourism Management, 26*, 815–832.

United Nations Environment Programme and World Tourism Organization. (2005). *Making tourism more sustainable: A guide for policy makers.* United Nations Environment Programme and World Tourism Organization.

Venkatesh, V., & Davis, F. D. (2000). A theoretical extension of the technology acceptance model: Four longitudinal field studies. *Management Science, 46*(2), 186–204.

Venkatesh, V., Morris, M. G., Davis, G. B., & Davis, F. D. (2003). User acceptance of information technology: Toward a unified view. *MIS Quarterly, 27*(3), 425–478.

Woodside, A. G., Krauss, E., Caldwell, M., & Chebat, J. C. (2007). Advancing theory for understanding travelers' own explanations of discretionary travel behavior. *Journal of Travel & Tourism Marketing, 22*(1), 15–35.

HETEROGENEITY IN TOURISM MOTIVATIONS: THE CASE OF THE ALGARVE

Jaime Serra, Antónia Correia and
Paulo M. M. Rodrigues

ABSTRACT

This chapter examines how motivational and behavioral indicators influence overnight stays of international tourists in the Algarve. The method includes a first selection of the motivations associating with high heterogeneity over the years considered, followed by a correlation matrix to assess how tourists' behavioral patterns relate with overnight stays. Behavioral patterns by year are defined based on motivations, socio-demographics, intentions, and lagged satisfaction. The correlation analysis was conducted using 15,542 observations collected at Faro international airport, from 2007 to 2010. The findings include 10 main motivations and reveal that these motivations are statistically different by country and over the years. This study contributes to the overall understanding of the dynamics of tourism demand.

Keywords: Algarve; demand; motivation; tourism; socio-demographics

Tourists' Behaviors and Evaluations
Advances in Culture, Tourism and Hospitality Research, Volume 9, 85–95
Copyright © 2014 by Emerald Group Publishing Limited
All rights of reproduction in any form reserved
ISSN: 1871-3173/doi:10.1108/S1871-317320140000009010

INTRODUCTION

Tourism is facing changes concerning the pattern of tourists' behavior. Further exploration and analysis of the effects of tourists' motivations and socio-demographic characteristics allows the tourism industry to understand what may explain the new patterns of international tourism demand. Despite the number of studies in the field of tourists' motivations, an approach for the understanding of the dynamic behavior of tourists' demand is still needed. However, it is possible to explain the dynamic nature of tourism demand at an individual level, for example, through motivations (Seeteram, 2010).

As Huang and Hsu (2009) argue, tourist motivations are a multidimensional construct able to explain tourists' choices, in a dynamic context. More than merely identifying tourist motivations it is vital to understand their influence in the choice process of international tourism travel as well as their dynamics. Tourists' socio-demographic characteristics represent additional dimensions important to consider when analyzing tourism demand. According to Heckman (2001), these variables account for heterogeneity in tourism behavior.

This study aims to identify the motivations, taking heterogeneity by country and by years into account, and to estimate the extent to which socio-demographic, motivational, and behavioral variables influence overnight stays of international tourists in the Algarve. This study contributes to the overall understanding of the dynamic patterns of tourism demand. In particular, this chapter provides empirical evidence on the influence of the combination of socio-demographic, behavioral, and motivational variables on over overnight stays.

THEORETICAL CONSIDERATIONS

Economic theory integrates income and price as main determinants in order to determine international tourism demand. However, noneconomic factors should also be considered (Crouch, 1994). Among several determinants and concerning consumer behavior theory, personal factors are related to socio-demographic characteristics of individuals. According to Saayman and Saayman (2009), socio-demographic variables can be used to explain travel behavior. Tourists' socio-demographic characteristics can be included as determinants of the demand to account for heterogeneity (Heckman, 2001).

Motivations for travel change over time and are influenced by past holiday experiences. Dann (1977, 1981) introduced the Pull and Push Theory of tourist motivations, which discussed and explained the factors that predispose a person to travel and those that attract the tourist to a given destination. The former are related to internal motives that explain why people travel (Crompton, 1979; Dann, 1977). Pull factors are related to external motives mainly exhorted by destination attributes (Crompton, 1979). Thus, motivations may be understood as the strength to practice a specific action and contain results of situation–person interactions (Gnoth, 1997). The role of motivations on travel behavior is emphasized by Mansfeld (1992), who alerts to the fact that two further problems exist to prevent the attainment of a reasonable theory that would enable the prediction of tourist behavior based on travel motivations. The first relates to the heterogeneity of the motives that trigger the decision to travel, and the second is the complex nature of travel motivations.

The relevant literature does not investigate deeply the changing patterns of behavior concerning tourist motivations. The patterns represent important information for destination stakeholders. Pearce and Stringer (1991) reveal that tourists can be very selective about how they relate their stories of travel, and extrinsic motives are usually prominent in the profile definition of motivation.

Past behavior at a destination is identifiable as one of the constructs of overall satisfaction and had a large combined effect on motivations (e.g., Huang & Hsu, 2009). Satisfaction associates sometimes with repeat visits (Kozak & Rimmington, 2000). Overall satisfaction and the number of prior visits influence return intention, especially in mature destinations (Kozak, 2001). Furthermore, according to the same author, destinations attributes influence future behavioral intentions and satisfaction which will lead to the likelihood of recommending and return intention.

HYPOTHESIS

As a result, the previous theoretical framework and literature review informs the construction of the following hypotheses:

H1. Socio-demographic characteristics are age, gender, marital status, level of education, income, employment status, and nationality associated with overnight stays.

H2. Travel companion correlate with overnight stays.

H3. Tourists' pull motivations over the years correlate with overnight stays.

H4. Past visits to a destination correlate with overnight stays.

H5. Overall satisfaction with past visits is positively correlated with overnight stays.

H6. Return intention to destination correlate with overnight stays.

H7. Individuals' attitudes in recommending a destination correlate with overnight stays.

METHOD

Following tourism demand studies in Algarve conducted by Correia and Crouch (2004), who find significant differences of perceptions and motivations of Algarve according to nationality, the present study is based on data provided by means of a questionnaire applied between 2007 and 2010, which was presented to a stratified, random sample of international tourists at their departure from Faro airport (Correia & Pimpão, 2012). The population of the study is matched to all international tourists visiting Algarve for the purpose of holidays/leisure, business, or visiting family and friends. Data comes from a project granted by ANA airports of Portugal that aims to monitor passengers and tourists. Questionnaires were administrated in the airport's departures lounge, and over the four years a sample of 15,542 tourists were interviewed. The sample size of 15,542 persons corresponding to a total of 2,636 questionnaires in 2007; 2,187 in 2008; 5,938 in 2009; and 4,781 in 2010 covers participants from age groups ranging from the less 20s to over 50 years. We also observed a wide variation in respondents' average household monthly income, which ranged from below 2,000 Euro to over 8,000 Euro. On average, the respondents belonged to the mid-age segment (the average age ranged from 31 to 50 years of age). A large portion of these respondents are married (more than 67%) and employed (63%) (Table 1).

In order to test the hypotheses, a correlation matrix was estimated by year (2007−2010) in order to identify whether overnight stays are correlated with socio-demographic variables such as nationality, age, gender,

Table 1. General Profile of Respondents, Sample Size, and Response Rate.

Variable Label	Unit	%
Socio-demographic		
Age		
<30	%	31.2
31–50	%	48.8
>51	%	20.0
Gender		
Male	%	46.3
Female	%	53.7
Marital status		
Married	%	67.3
Single	%	29.9
Divorced/widowed	%	2.8
Education		
Elementary	%	22.5
Secondary	%	75.9
University	%	1.6
Monthly income		
<€2,000	%	15.7
€2,001–€3,500	%	22.4
€3,501–€5,000	%	40.8
€5,001–€8,000	%	10.9
>€8,001	%	10.2
Work situation		
Employed	%	62.3
Unemployed	%	22.0
Not active	%	9.3
Student	%	5.0
Retired	%	1.4
Nationality		
The United Kingdom	%	29.8
Germany	%	24.2
The Netherlands	%	5.3
Ireland	%	18.1
Scandinavia (Norway, Denmark, Sweden, Finland)	%	8.9
Others	%	13.7
Past visit behavior	%	46.6
First time visit	%	53.4

Table 1.   (*Continued*)

Variable Label	Unit	%
Travel companion		
Alone	%	9.6
Spouse/family	%	73.0
Friends/group	%	16.8
Other	%	0.6
Return intention		
No	%	48.0
Yes	%	52.0
Recommendation		
No	%	55.5
Yes	%	44.5
N (number of respondents)		15,542

marital status, education, income, work situation, travel companion, past behavior visit, overall satisfaction, return intention, recommendation, and pull motivations, such as, cleanliness, cultural, and historical resources, information available, closeness to home, accommodation, gastronomy, price, hospitality, sightseeing and excursions, and golf facilities. Assuming that tourist motivations are heterogeneous, the Scheffé test was used to test for significant differences by year. The results confirmed differences in tourist motivations across the years. The previous tourist motivations considered were the motivations that present more variability over the years under analysis.

FINDINGS

This section presents the results based on the correlation matrix which appears in Table 2. After estimation of the correlation matrix, the variables that are correlated with overnight stays were identified.

According to the hypotheses and their theoretical framework, the findings suggest the following conclusions. Regarding the variables of socio-demographic characteristics, differences across the years are identified between nationalities, work situation status, age, gender, level of education, and marital status. Concerning marital status, in 2007 ($r = 0.043$), 2009

Table 2. Correlation Matrix.

		Overnights	Country	Past Behavior	Travel Companion	Cleanliness	Closeness to Home	Price	Sightseeing and Excursions	Return Intention	Recommendation	Gender	Age	Marital	Education	Work Situation
Overnights 2010	Pearson	1	-0.001	-0.153**	-0.081**	-0.019	0.014	-0.075**	-0.051**	-0.069**	-0.010	0.041**	0.083**	0.064**	-0.031*	-0.040**
	correlation sig. (two-tailed)		0.953	0.000	0.000	0.191	0.337	0.000	0.000	0.000	0.474	0.005	0.000	0.000	0.030	0.006
Overnights 2009	Pearson	1	-0.052**	-0.115**	-0.056**	0.034**	0.027*	-0.013	-0.007	-0.049**	-0.016	0.007	0.093**	0.039**	-0.015	-0.064**
	correlation sig. (two-tailed)		0.000	0.000	0.000	0.010	0.040	0.308	0.591	0.000	0.214	0.590	0.000	0.003	0.255	0.000
Overnights 2008	Pearson	1	-0.006	-0.105**	-0.138**	0.001	-0.033	-0.030	-0.010	-0.064**	0.025	0.026	0.051*	0.031	-0.013	-0.037
	correlation sig. (two-tailed)		0.788	0.000	0.000	0.969	0.119	0.167	0.632	0.003	0.238	0.217	0.017	0.151	0.532	0.084
Overnights 2007	Pearson	1	0.009	-0.041*	0.002	-0.018	-0.047*	-0.014	0.031	-0.019	0.046*	-0.021	0.075**	0.043*	-0.054**	
	correlation sig. (two-tailed)		0.642	0.037	0.923	0.351	0.017	0.479	0.109	0.321	0.018	0.276	0.000	0.026	0.005	

*Correlation is significant at the 0.05 level (two-tailed).
**Correlation is significant at the 0.01 level (two-tailed).

($r = 0.039$), and 2010 ($r = 0.064$), a positive correlation which may suggest that the Algarve is a destination sought after by couples and families, which is in accordance with Correia and Crouch (2004). These findings are presented in Table 2 and according to the theoretical and empirical context considered, *hypothesis 1 is not rejected.*

Concerning travel companion, in 2008 ($r = -0.138$), 2009 ($r = -0.056$), and 2010 ($r = -0.081$), a negative correlation with overnight stays is observed. Since the Algarve is considered a sun and sand family destination and also contains a considerable amount of repeaters, negative correlation results suggest that tourists' dependables profile tends to stay for shorter periods of time over the years (Plog, 2001). Decreasing patterns of this variable may be justified by Alegre, Mateo, and Pou (2011, p. 558) who remark that this could be a "consequence of the individuals' time and financial constraints and of other demographic and socioeconomic characteristics that determine their preference for a 'short' or 'long' holiday." According to the theoretical and empirical context considered H2 receives support.

Concerning tourists' motivations results seem to suggest different patterns of correlation on overnight stays in the Algarve. According to the findings of Correia and Crouch (2004), sun and sand are the predominant leading choice attributes among tourists in the Algarve. However, assuming this implicit destination attribute, the present research focuses on the motivations that evidence more variability. Hence, cleanliness associates positively with overnight stays ($r = 0.034$); closeness to home in 2007 associates negatively with overnight stays (−0.47), however in 2009 shifts to a positive correlation ($r = 0.027$); price ($r = -0.075$), sightseeing and excursions ($r = -0.051$) is negatively correlated with overnight stays. These results suggest that in fact over the years the motivations are changing, which are in line with recent findings in tourism motivations studies (e.g., Pearce & Lee, 2005), which explains how motivations change. Accordingly, motivational factors are present over the years, however, only cleanliness, closeness to home, price, and sightseeing and excursions motivations are significant. Hence, according the above results, H3 is partially not rejected.

Correlation matrix results show the significance of past behavior in all years. However, it is negatively correlated (e.g., for 2010 $r = -0.153$) with overnight stays, which suggests that repeat visitors tend to spend less time at destinations than in their first visit. Results are in line with Oppermann (1996), who observes that repeated visitors tend to spend less time than a first time visitor. Hence, from the regression results, H4 is not rejected.

Although overall satisfaction was considered in the correlation estimation is not significant in any of the years considered. A possible reason is that some other variables considered in the model, which can be assumed as proxies for satisfaction (return intention and recommendation), are significant in some of the years. Thus, considering the above results H5 is rejected.

The return intention is significant in some of the years. However, results may indicate that revisiting intentions is negatively correlated (year 2008 $r = -0.064$, and year 2010 $r = -0.069$) with overnight stays in the Algarve. Although return intentions could be evidence of a certain degree of loyalty (Oppermann, 2000), first time visitors in the Algarve tend to spend more time rather than repeat visitors. In view of the above results, H6 is partially not rejected. Recommendation behavior presents a positive correlation with overnight stays ($r = 0.046$) in the Algarve, although this is only observed for one year and the finding is significant only for 2007. Thus, H7 is partially not rejected.

CONCLUSION AND IMPLICATIONS

This research presents several theoretical contributions. The study confirms that noneconomic antecedents contribute to explaining international tourism demand. This conclusion is in line with the findings of Cho (2010). Another contribution concerns international tourism demand models which are commonly based on classical economic theory. Thus, introducing behavioral and motivational factors could help in the better understanding of tourists' choice behavior. The findings confirm the assumptions provided by Papatheodorou (2001) who highlighted and warned against the fact that the use of traditional demand theory in tourism suffers from a number of serious drawbacks, since it ignores specific particularities of tourism products.

Concerning the contribution to the scope of behavioral and motivational theories, findings on the return intention variable confirmed that it can be significant when isolated from the issue of satisfaction. Indeed present findings also confirmed the statement of theories of human behavior (Sonmez & Graefe, 1998), which suggests that past behavior is a good predictor of behavioral intention and actual future behavior. Thus, the correlation of past behavior of international tourists in Algarve negatively influences overnight stays. Tourist motivations in Algarve present heterogeneous patterns over the years and confirm the conclusions that motivations change over time put forward by Pearce and Lee (2005). Therefore, tourists' motivations for sun and sand destinations are dynamic and present differences on the influence of overnight stays when combined with nationalities. This study estimates the extent to which motivational, behavioral, and socio-demographic factors influence overnight stays of the main international tourism markets in the Algarve. In order to test several hypotheses, the results showed that a combination of socio-demographic, motivational, and behavioral factors influence overnight stays. Hence, the results presented confirm the dynamic pattern of tourist behavior, that is, the variables that influence overnight stays differ over the years considered. Results provided by the correlation matrix across the years indicate that not all motivations reveal a significant influence on overnight stays. Those found significant were sightseeing and excursions, cleanliness, closeness to home, and price. An interesting finding is related to the dynamic pattern of tourist motivations, which appear with changing patterns over the years. This last finding is useful for tourism management authorities in order to adequate the typical sun and sand product of the Algarve to the pattern of other tourist motivations. Future studies concerning the heterogeneous pattern of tourist motivations are necessary in order to understand the heterogeneous characteristics of international tourism demand. Furthermore, exploring and ranking travel motivations is an interesting issue that needs to be addressed in order to identify turning points in tourist preferences and consequently to better understand tourist destination choice behavior.

ACKNOWLEDGMENT

The authors thank the 8th CPTHL scientific committee for useful comments and suggestions on an earlier version of this chapter.

REFERENCES

Alegre, J., Mateo, S., & Pou, L. (2011). A latent class approach to tourists' length of stay. *Tourism Management, 32*(3), 555–563.

Cho, V. (2010). A study of the non-economic determinants in tourism demand. *International Journal of Tourism Research, 12*, 307–320.

Correia, A., & Crouch, G. I. (2004). Tourist perceptions of and motivations for visiting the Algarve, Portugal. *Tourism Analysis, 8*(2–4), 165–169.

Correia, A., & Pimpão, A. (2012). Initiative monitoring report. Unpublished report. Faro, University of Algarve.

Crompton, J. L. (1979). Motivations for pleasure vacation. *Annals of Tourism Research, 6*(4), 408–424.

Crouch, G. I. (1994). The study of international tourism demand: A review of findings. *Journal of Travel Research, 33*(1), 12–23.

Dann, G. (1977). Anomie, ego-enhancement and tourism. *Annals of Tourism Research, 4*(4), 184–194.

Dann, G. (1981). Tourist motivation: An appraisal. *Annals of Tourism Research, 8*(2), 187–219.

Gnoth, J. (1997). Tourism motivation and expectation formation. *Annals of Tourism Research, 24*(2), 283–304.

Heckman, J. J. (2001). Micro data, heterogeneity, and the evaluation of public policy: Nobel lecture. *Journal of Political Economy, 109*(4), 673–748.

Huang, S., & Hsu, C. H. C. (2009). Effects of travel motivation, past experience, perceived constraint, and attitude on revisit intention. *Journal of Travel Research, 48*(1), 29–44.

Kozak, M. (2001). Comparative assessment of tourist satisfaction with destination across two nationalities. *Tourism Management, 22*(4), 391–401.

Kozak, M., & Rimmington, N. (2000). Tourist satisfaction with Mallorca, Spain, as an off-season holiday destination. *Journal of Travel Research, 38*(3), 260–269.

Mansfeld, Y. (1992). From motivation to actual travel. *Annals of Tourism Research, 19*(3), 399–419.

Oppermann, M. (1996). Convention destination images: Analysis of association meeting planners' perceptions. *Tourism Management, 17*(3), 175–182.

Oppermann, M. (2000). Tourism destination loyalty. *Journal of Travel Research, 39*(1), 78–84.

Papatheodorou, A. (2001). Why people travel to different places. *Annals of Tourism Research, 28*(1), 164–179.

Pearce, P. L., & Lee, U. (2005). Developing the travel career approach to tourist motivation. *Journal of Travel Research, 43*(3), 226–237.

Pearce, P. L., & Stringer, P. F. (1991). Psychology and tourism. *Annals of Tourism Research, 18*(1), 136–154.

Plog, S. (2001). Why destination areas rise and fall in popularity: An update of a cornell quarterly classic. *Cornell Hotel and Restaurant Administration Quarterly, 42*(3), 13–24.

Saayman, M., & Saayman, A. (2009). Why travel motivation and socio-demographic matter in managing a national park. *Koedoe, 51*(1), 1–9.

Seeteram, N. (2010). Use of dynamic panel cointegration approach to model international arrivals to Australia. *Journal of Travel Research, 49*(4), 414–422.

Sonmez, S., & Graefe, A. (1998). Determining future travel behavior from past travel experience and perceptions of risk and safety. *Journal of Travel Research, 37*(4), 171–177.

CONFIGURAL MODELING OF COUNTRY-COLLECTORS MOTIVES, BEHAVIOR, AND ASSESSMENTS OF STRENGTHS OF NATIONAL-PLACE BRANDS

Arch G. Woodside, Xiang (Robert) Li and Karlan Muniz

ABSTRACT

"Country-collectors" (CCs) are defined here as international leisure travelers who have visited 6 + countries within the five most recent calendar years primarily to pursue leisure activities. The study here contributes by offering an early workbench model of antecedents, paths, and outcomes of country-collectors' evaluations and behavior toward countries as place-brands competing for such visitors. This study reports findings from a large-scale omnibus survey in three large Japanese cities (total n = 1,200). *Key findings support the model and the following conclusions. Generally, country-collectors represent a small share of a nation's adult population (less than 5%) but over 40% of the total leisure trips abroad; country-collectors are classifiable into distinct sub-segments according to*

Tourists' Behaviors and Evaluations
Advances in Culture, Tourism and Hospitality Research, Volume 9, 97–133
Copyright © 2014 by Emerald Group Publishing Limited
ISSN: 1871-3173/doi:10.1108/S1871-317320140000009011

the country place-brands that they visit; CC sub-segments, less frequent international leisure travelers, and stay-in-country travelers and non-travelers each offer unique assessments of competing countries as place-brands. National place-brand strategists planning a marketing campaign to influence a given nation's residents to visit a specific destination (e.g., persuading Japanese nationals to visit the United States) may increase the campaign's effectiveness by using this workbench model. The study offers a blueprint of how to appraise strengths and weaknesses of competing national place-brands among realized and potential visitors in specific national markets.

Keywords: Country-collectors; leisure; Japanese; place-brands; travel

INTRODUCTION

Collecting includes the acquisition of material objects, ideas, or experiences (e.g., travel, restaurant, or concert experiences, with or without tangible manifestations of these experiences) that includes many-to-all of the following characteristics: collections seldom begin purposively; addiction and compulsive aspects pervade collecting; collecting legitimizes acquisitiveness as art or science; profane to sacred conversions occur when an item enters a collection (cf. Belk, 1995). Collections serve as extensions of self; collections tend toward specializations (not all collectors are alike); post-mortem distribution problems are significant to collectors and their families; there is a simultaneous desire for and fear of completing a collection (Belk, Wallendorf, Sherry, Holbrook, & Roberts, 1988). In a limited geographic sense crossing imaginary geographic lines (e.g., the Arctic Circle and the Equator), Timothy (1998) introduces the expression, "collecting places." King and Prideaux (2010) examine the collection of World Heritage protected areas, as a tourism behavior, using a specific case study in Queensland. Then, a very limited amount of additional research refers to or explores the concept.

The present study expands the concept, offers an exploratory theory of antecedents and outcomes of country collecting, and examines that theory using a large-scale survey of Japanese country-collectors versus noncollectors who visit international destinations, and domestic only travelers and non-travelers. Both the theory and empirical findings support three key conclusions. First, the share of revenue country-collectors provided is very substantial relative to their small share of a country's population. Second, few-to-many country-collectors are identifiable in all income, age, education levels, and living in smaller versus very large cities. Third, unique sub-segments of country-collectors are identifiable by nations visited and motivations to visit these destinations.

Given that one of the best seller books (1st in sales in the *New York Times* ranking) is *1,000 Places to See Before You Die* (Schultz, 2010) and that "travel the world" ranks number one on the "bucket list" among adult men and women, according to recent studies (Waterlow, 2012), the study here raises and answers the following important questions. Do country-collectors exist? If they do exist, who are they? What motivates them? How do they judge major national travel-destination brands such as Australia, mainland China, France, Italy, the United Kingdom, South Korea, and the United States?

Following this introduction, section "Country-Collectors' Definition and Importance in the Marketplace" proposes that the "country collector" concept relates to the "heavy-half" principle, that is, 80% of the volume is consumed by 20% of the users of the product or service (Twedt, 1964) – or more generally, less that 20% of users are identifiable as very frequent users and these highly frequent users account for 40–60% of the total consumption of the product or service category (Woodside, Cook, & Mindak, 1987). Section "A Theory for Explaining Antecedents, Processes, and Outcomes of country-collectors' Behavior" describes an exploratory model that includes potential antecedent influences on country collecting behavior and resulting outcomes of such behavior. Section "Method" describes the method of an empirical study that permits exploration of the model. Section "Results" presents findings from the empirical study. Section "Conclusions, Limitations, and Implications" concludes with implications, limitations, and suggestions for future country collector studies.

The idea and activity of collecting has been around since the dawn of mankind. Initially, humans (as well as animals) collected food and other necessities as security against rainy days (Belk, 1982). While that might still be the case in some parts of world today, most customers in industrialized countries now collect nonnecessities for leisure, non-utilitarian purposes (Belk, 1988; McIntosh & Schmeichel, 2004). As a nearly universal human activity, collecting is viewed as a form of serious leisure (Case, 2009; Stebbins, 2004a, 2004b) and "materialistic luxury consumption par excellence" (Belk, 1995, p. 479).

Belk (1995, p. 67) defined collecting as "the process of actively, selectively, and passionately acquiring and possessing things removed from ordinary use and perceived as part of a set of non-identical objects or experiences." He further suggests that collecting distinguishes from most other consumption behaviors in "the concern for a set of objects, the passion invested in obtaining and maintaining these objects, and the lack of ordinary uses to which these collected objects are put" (Belk, 1995, p. 67).

A collector is "a person who is motivated to accumulate a series of similar objects where the instrumental function of the objects is of secondary (or no) concern and the person does not plan to immediately dispose of the objects" (McIntosh & Schmeichel, 2004, p. 86). Belk (1991) suggests there are at least two types of collectors: the taxonomic collectors, such as coin or post stamp collectors, whose goal is to own an example of every unit of a set of items produced; and the *aesthetic* collectors, such as art collectors, whose attempt to gather many pleasing examples of certain items (Case, 2009). Notably, for the former group, set completion has been argued to be one important motivation to collect (Carey, 2008). Other market research revealed four types of collectors: passionate collectors, acquisitive collectors, hobbyists, and expressive collectors (Saari, 1997). Indeed, from achieving immortality to traumatic healing (Feller, 2011), researchers have identified a large number of sociological, psychological, economic, even biological reasons behind why people engage in collecting activities (McIntosh & Schmeichel, 2004). Arguably, most of these motivations appear to revolve around the self (McIntosh & Schmeichel, 2004). That is, collecting helps define and complete collectors' identities, and the collection may reflect one's "extended self" (Belk, 1988).

In terms what may be collected, Case (2009, p. 732) reviews the literature on collectibles and concluded that "*anything* is collectible." In the similar vein, Carey (2008, p. 338) also asserts that "virtually anything can lend itself to collecting." Nevertheless, a closer look at the literature suggests that most previous studies focused only on goods, while experience collecting has drawn little scholarly attention (Keinan & Kivetz, 2011). Considering the central role experience plays in today's economy (Pine & Gilmore, 1998, 1999), particularly to the tourism industry (Tung & Ritchie, 2011), this study attempts to fill this gap in the tourism literature. Specifically, this study examines experience collectors through destination (country) collection.

COUNTRY-COLLECTORS' DEFINITION AND IMPORTANCE IN THE MARKETPLACE

Some researchers explore the segmentation of markets to identify consumer niches in tourism, evaluating geographic, demographic and psychographic characteristics, expenditure, benefits, activities, and communication; for a summary of studies on tourist segmentation, see Jang, Morrison, and O'Leary (2002). Segmenting the market provides a more accurate understanding of the characteristics, motivation, and behavior of a given group, enabling better offers and more effective communication (Jang et al., 2002; Kotler & Keller, 2009). The present study starts off with a classification according to the number of countries visited recently (the past five years) and the result is the identification of a segment of heavy users, known as country-collectors.

"Country-collectors" (CCs) are defined here to be international leisure travelers who have visited 6 + countries within the five more recent calendar years primarily to pursue leisure activities. Building on Belk's (1995) definition of collecting, Keinan and Kivetz (2011, p. 937) define the collection of experiences as "the process of actively and selectively acquiring memorable experiences as a part of a set of non-identical experiences." Their study concludes that a productivity orientation − to use time productively in order to achieve accomplishments − can intensify the consumption of unusual or different collectible experiences, including the choice of places to go on vacation (countries), leisure activities and celebrations, even though, in some cases, these are not exactly the choices that provide the most pleasure.

Ratner, Kahn, and Kahneman (1999) describe how subjects may prefer variety when consuming products and services hedonistically with a view to maximizing utility during consumption even if the derived pleasure is less than that of previously consumed hedonistic product. According to Keinan and Kivetz (2011), consumers build up opportunities to be productive and construct an "experiential CV." When it comes to tourism and trips abroad, novelty or variety seeking has long been revealed as a key travel motivation (Lee & Crompton, 1992; Petrick, 2002; Snepenger, 1987). Presumably, studying a segment that prioritizes the variety of countries visited can broaden our understanding of the motivation and behavior of this group.

Fig. 1 describes the membership and share of the CC segment in the present study. The smallest segment of people (under 16% of the total) includes those who have visited six or more countries in the past five years. However, they are responsible for 42% of the total number of international trips during the period in question.

A segment with this volume of trips and this behavior suggests great potential for substantial profits. For instance, Fig. 2 shows that country-collectors' interest in traveling abroad has the higher priority in comparison with the other segments under study (significant mean differences were

4 Groups (According to Number of Countries Visited Past 5 Years)	Mean of Trips	n	% Pop Travelers	Number of Trips	%
No countries visited	0.00	600		0	0.00
One to two countries visited	1.36	324	54.00	442	22.7
Three to five countries visited	3.77	182	30.33	687	35.3
Six or more countries visited	8.70	94	15.67	818	42.0
Total	1.62	1200	100.00	1947	100
			Travelers n = 600		

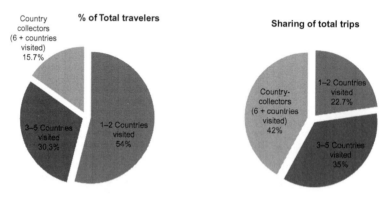

Fig. 1. The Country-Collectors' Segment.

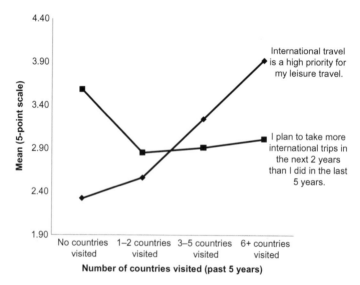

Fig. 2. Importance of International Travel and Future Intention Comparison to the Past, about Taking International Trips. *Notes*: Five-point scales used from strongly disagree to strongly agree. Significant difference (> 0.4 difference) in means comparison (ANOVA tests). Importance of international travel ($F = 92.741$; $p < 0.001$; eta$^2 = 0.19$) and future intentions about taking international trips ($F = 39.930$; $p < 0.001$; eta$^2 = 0.094$).

found), and that they show a high degree of willingness to make more international trips in the near future.

A THEORY FOR EXPLAINING ANTECEDENTS, PROCESSES, AND OUTCOMES OF COUNTRY-COLLECTORS' BEHAVIOR

This section proposes a model that seeks to provide details of the consumer behavior of country-collectors. Fig. 3 summarizes a sample of a set of specific characteristics of country-collectors, their reasons for visiting certain countries, and their behavior. Similar to the proposals by Twedt (1964), the composition of this group of people who enjoy visiting and "trying out" new countries is not obvious from examining demographic characteristics such as household income or age. Therefore, in addition to specific analyses regarding their socioeconomic characteristics, there are also analyses using a set-theory for building and testing causal recipes

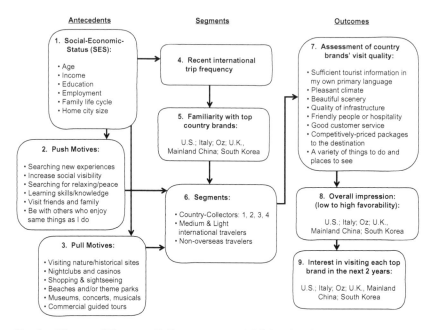

Fig. 3. Theory of Country-Collectors versus Additional Leisure Travel Segments.

(i.e., conjunctive statements that predict high scores in country collecting), with a view to proposing and testing alternative profiles sufficient to identify this segment. Variables concerning socioeconomic status (SES) and motivation or facilitating features that lead this group to travel for leisure are tested. The study here examines the activities that most attract this group to travel for leisure.

Other analyses seek to describe micro-segments among heavy users, seeking explanation concerning the behavior of travelers according to the number of trips abroad recently and their degree of familiarity with different countries. The CC segment is divisible into different sub-groups, which this study accomplishes according to the places they have visited.

In an attempt to contrast the behavior and perception of the CC segment in comparison to other leisure travelers and connect their attitude to future behavior, the study examines country-collectors' perceptions and opinions regarding the specific attributes of countries, along with their general impressions and interest and whether they intend to visit these countries in the coming years.

METHOD

Data Source

The data used in this study are from a large, two-phase project examining Japan's US-bound travel market. A total of 1,200 online panel surveys were completed by Japanese nationals aged 18 years or older. Survey respondents include a sample ($n = 600$) of outbound travelers – people who traveled overseas in the past 5 years – and a sample ($n = 600$) of future outbound travelers – people who did not travel overseas in the past 5 years but intend to do so in the next 2 years.

The quota sampling approach involved the equal division among three major cities (three samples of 400 participants from each city including Nagoya, Osaka, and Tokyo). The segmentations in the planning of the sample enabled contrasts to be drawn between the characteristics and perceptions of those who had already traveled in recent years and who had not.

Comparisons could also be drawn between cities of different sizes. The survey collected a wide range of information including SES, number of trips, a mention of the countries visited, questions regarding the reasons for traveling and interest in specific activities, overall impression of countries, and comparisons of countries based on perceptions of specific attributes, future intentions and specific questions about the United States, and competing destinations for Japanese visitors. Multiple rounds of pilot tests were completed with the survey before the main study.

Analysis

Following the preliminary analysis of the characteristics as number of trips and the number of countries visited in the past 5 years, the segment of CC was identified. Using traditional statistics analysis (chi-square and ANOVA), some characteristics and perceptions were compared. To improve the analysis and find out the characteristics that best describe country-collectors, this study also applies qualitative comparative analysis (QCA) (Ragin, 2008), rather than only calculating the net effects of independent variables in linear models from a symmetric (correlation and multiple regression) perspective.

QCA is a method that bridges quantitative and qualitative methods (Ragin, 2008). According to Ragin (2008), most theoretical arguments of social science concern set-theoretic relationships, not linear relationships between variables. Set-theoretical connections are asymmetrical rather than symmetrical. Using Boolean algebra, QCA examines cases with their different causally relevant conditions. The present study describes complex antecedent conditions (social-economic status and situational/motivational statements) that profile CC sub-segments in a more useful manner than multiple regression analysis. Validation by applying combinations of matrix algebra based statistical analysis with Boolean algebra QCA analysis may be less elegant, but it is more informative than the use of either alone (Woodside & Zhang, 2012).

According to Ragin (2008), an especially useful feature of QCA is its capacity for analyzing complex causation, a situation in which an outcome may follow from several different combinations of casual condition, that is, different "recipes" lead to high scores on the outcome condition whereby the outcome condition in this study is a high CC membership score. In the study of country-collectors, it is expected that there is not just one configurational condition of antecedents but rather several alternative "recipes" for the outcome of being a CC.

Two important concepts emerge from using QCA: the set-theoretic consistency determines the degree to which the cases sharing particular combinations of conditions (for instance, in this study, the SES and reasons to travel) agree regarding the outcome in question (i.e., CC membership). Set-theoretic coverage evaluates the degree to which a casual combination accounts for instances of an outcome (Ragin, 2008). According to additional studies testing causal recipes using configural comparative analysis, this method is worth pursuing in research on explaining and modeling international tourism behavior (e.g., Woodside, Hsu, & Marshall, 2011).

RESULTS

Antecedents of Country-Collectors' Behavior

From traditional statistical analyses, country-collectors are found among every age group, at every level of household income, city size, employment status, and level of education. Details of the demographic breakouts do not appear due to the confidentiality of the information requirements of the sponsors of the study. Five percent or more of each of six age segments are country-collectors with the 60−69 age segment having the greatest share of country-collectors (13%). In analyzing household income, all the different stages have at least 3% of country-collectors, while the group between 9 to 12 million yen (approximately, 80−120 thousand USD) has 10% and the group above this level has more than 17% Country-Collectors. The comparison among cities shows that the largest center (Tokyo, with almost nine million inhabitants) has a larger portion of country-collectors (12%) than Nagoya (2.3 million inhabitants and 6.8% of country-collectors) and Osaka (2.7 million inhabitants and 4.8% of country-collectors).

Regarding employment status, a slightly higher proportion of country-collectors were found among retired and self-employed people (11% and 9%, respectively), while, when talking about levels of education, most country-collectors are either university graduates or have an even higher level of education (11% and 15.6% of these groups are country-collectors).

The tables and comparisons presented, however, are insufficient for accurate prediction that a participant is CC. Therefore, beyond the preliminary analysis, QCA was used to profile high membership scores in being a CC. Calibration of the antecedents was performed (analogous to Z-score transformations in statistical analysis) and the same independent variables (such as SES and others push motives for traveling overseas) were tested in order to find a consistent set of casual conditions. To be more accurate in this analysis, the QCA analyses focus on the sample of prior overseas travelers ($n = 600$).

The QCA method helps to identify causal recipes (Ragin, 2008) and captures the conjoining of specific scores of two or more simple antecedent conditions. The first analysis uses the number of trips overseas in the past five years as the outcome condition — calibrated membership from 0 to 1.0. Table 1 presents the causal recipes in the resulting complex solution, with accurate levels of coverage and consistency.

Different causal recipes can represent accurate paths for a high CC membership — 6 + countries visited in overseas travel during the past five years. For instance, if on the one hand the recipe that includes high income, high education, and living in a big city (algorithm 5 of Table 1) is an accurate causal recipe for CC membership, a low level of income in combination with a high level of age (algorithm 3 of the Table 1) also represents a second accurate path in high CC membership. (The mid-level "*" is the logical "and" condition in Table 1 and QCA generally — a set-theory analysis step analogous to an interaction term in statistical analysis).

Table 2 shows additional configural conditions that result in a high score on the number of countries visited (outcome condition). High CC membership results in complex antecedent configuration that include high scores in income and education, both at high levels and connected with high levels of age or bigger home cities (algorithms 4 and 5), and low levels and associated with high levels of age (algorithm 3). But if the socioeconomic profile cannot in itself fully account for becoming a CC, including additional simple antecedents may increase accuracy in predicting CC membership.

Table 1. Fuzzy Set QCA for High Score on Number of Trips.

Algorithm	Model	Raw Coverage	Unique Coverage	Consistency
1	~inc_c*~retired_c	0.693	0.111	0.737
2	educ_c*~ retired_c	0.616	0.066	0.826
3	~inc_c*age_c	0.438	0.020	0.867
4	educ_c*age_c	0.362	0.006	0.904
5	inc_c*educ_c*city_sz_c	0.222	0.001	0.963

Notes: Solution coverage: 0.919358; solution consistency: 0.735558; sample includes 600 respondents (only participants who traveled 5 past years).

Table 2. Fuzzy Set QCA for High Score on Countries Visited.

Algorithm	Model	Raw Coverage	Unique Coverage	Consistency
1	~retired_c*~inc_c	0.746	0.090	0.631
2	~retired_c*educ_c	0.659	0.058	0.703
3	age_c*~educ_c*~inc_c	0.394	0.023	0.827
4	age_c*educ_c*inc_c	0.323	0.005	0.919
5	city_sz_c*educ_c*inc_c	0.266	0.001	0.915

Notes: Solution coverage: 0.934506; sample includes 600 (only participants who have traveled 5 past years).

In order to broaden the analysis, the study included learning the principle motivations for overseas traveling a leisure trip. The objective was to combine SES with specific reasons to travel. Using exploratory factor analysis, six dimensions were identified among the 19 items describing reasons to travel. The six factors include seeking new experiences, increasing social visibility, seeking relaxation/peace, learning skills and knowledge, visiting friends and family, and being with others who enjoy same thing. Some of these dimensions (novelty seeking, escape/relaxation seeking, learning, prestige and family) appear in other studies on Japanese travelers (Andersen, Prentice, & Watanabe, 2000; Cha, McCleary, & Uysal, 1995; Jang et al., 2002).

From ANOVA tests, the CC segment had means that are significantly higher versus other segments for three dimensions for "visiting friends and family" ($F = 9.833$; $p < 0.001$), "seeking new experiences" ($F = 8.612$; $p < 0.001$), and "learning skills and abilities" ($F = 4.206$; $p = 0.015$). Thus, including these motivations in the analysis can offer a broader understanding of country-collectors' antecedents.

The solutions from QCA include additional and still highly consistent paths indicating high CC membership scores. Table 3 reveals that the association of the variable "visiting friends and family" with the socioeconomic variables provide greater terms of explanation to the resulting solution. For instance, the subject may not appear to have a high income level, but being of a more advanced age and having a high level of education and friends and family overseas increases the possibility of his or her becoming a Country Collector (algorithm 5 in the solution, Table 3). Without the presence of friends/family, the level of income or the size of the home city becomes an informative antecedent condition factor (algorithms 6 and 7).

However, algorithm 4 in Table 3 presents a QCA model that includes no friends/family, low levels of education and income, and high levels of age

Table 3. Fuzzy Set QCA for High Score on Number of Countries Visited.

Algorithm	Model	Raw Coverage	Unique Coverage	Consistency
1	~retired_c*~inc_c	0.746	0.116	0.631
2	~retired_c*educ_c	0.659	0.074	0.702
3	age_c*city_sz_c*educ_c	0.212	0.006	0.858
4	~vis_frds_c*age_c*~educ_c*~inc_c	0.343	0.021	0.874
5	vis_frds_c*age_c*educ_c*~inc_c	0.217	0.001	0.943
6	~vis_frds_c*age_c*educ_c*inc_c	0.274	0.004	0.938
7	~vis_frds_c*city_sz_c*educ_c*inc_c	0.208	0.001	0.950

Notes: Solution coverage: 0.941773; solution consistency: 0.608392; sample includes 600 respondents indicating travel overseas in prior 5 years.

that results in CC membership. According to the algorithm 5 in Table 3, we can infer that the presence of friends and family can itself to be an alternative for a tourist to become a CC, although she/he does not have the necessary income for such membership. This specific recipe in algorithm 5 achieves high levels of raw coverage (0.217) and a very high level of consistency of prediction of CC membership (0.943).

Fig. 4 shows the plot of a causal recipe that includes "visiting friends and family*high age*high education*low income" and the outcome of being high in CC membership. In the plot, the X axis represents the combination of low income, visiting friends and family, higher age, and higher education, and the Y axis means the amount of countries visited. Fig. 4 shows most cases either above the main diagonal or near it. The CC cases with high membership scores on the outcome are all in the upper triangle, indicating a high consistency scores for high sufficiency, which means the most part of the sample follow this pattern. See the appendix for a discussion and visual on the meaning of sufficiency.

However, exploring additional antecedents can help to clarify additional explanations of the antecedents of being a Country Collector. For example, adding the reasons to travel (pull factors, such as "experience something different" from the "seeking new experiences" dimension) in Table 4 clarifies that this goal can be important when connected to some demographic and economic antecedents, and that this antecedent can be decisive in the absence of friends and family in the destination countries (algorithms 8–11 of Table 4) and vice versa (algorithm 11 of Table 4). These algorithms have informative levels of raw coverage (most are above 0.2) and informative levels of consistency (most are above 0.85).

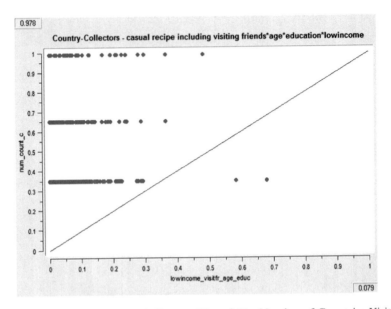

Fig. 4. XY Plot for Country-Collectors. Plot of Y = Number of Countries Visited by X = Combined Causal Configuration (Visiting Friends/Family*Age*Education* Low Income).

Table 4. Fuzzy Set QCA for High Score on Number of Countries Visited.[a]

Algorithm	Model	Raw Coverage	Unique Coverage	Consistency
1	exp_something_d*~retired_c*~inc_c	0.727	0.054	0.689
2	exp_something_d*~retired_c*educ_c	0.640	0.055	0.741
3	~age_c*~city_sz_c*~retired_c*~inc_c	0.420	0.001	0.694
4	~vis_frds_c*age_c*~city_sz_c*~educ_c*~inc_c	0.246	0.015	0.874
5	~vis_frds_c*~age_c*~retired_c*educ_c*~inc_c	0.374	0.001	0.847
6	vis_frds_c*~age_c*~city_sz_c*~retired_c*educ_c	0.207	0.002	0.856
7	~vis_frds_c*age_c*~city_sz_c*~retired_c*educ_c	0.200	0.001	0.881
8	exp_something_d*~vis_frds_c*age_c*city_sz_c*~inc_c	0.204	0.010	0.901
9	exp_something_d*~vis_frds_c*age_c*educ_c*inc_c	0.273	0.004	0.941
10	exp_something_d*~vis_frds_c*city_sz_c*educ_c*inc_c	0.207	0.001	0.951
11	exp_something_d*age_c*city_sz_c*educ_c*inc_c	0.182	0.001	0.951
12	~exp_something_d*vis_frds_c*age_c*retired_c*educ_c*~inc_c	0.013	0.002	0.805

Notes: Solution coverage: 0.925638; solution consistency: 0.653758; here, we have five social-economic status variables (income, age, education, retired, city size) and two reasons to travel (visit friends and family, experience something different); sample includes 600 respondents indicating travel overseas in prior 5 years.
[a]Intermediate solution. Function Model: num_count_c = f(exp_something_d, vis_frds_c, age_c, city_sz_c, retired_c, educ_c, inc_c).

The plot in Fig. 5 exemplifies the recipe combination among people who have higher income, age, and education, and who are not visiting friends and family. As a push motive, these people want to experience something different. By combining all these conditions, a person can be (or become) a CC.

Putting together the three main reasons to travel that differentiate the country-collectors from the other traveler segments, and combining the socioeconomic characteristics, some solutions, some different recipes, can explain the outcome of the number of countries visited, according to findings in Table 5. For instance, people with high levels of education and income, from a big city, with low age and no friends/family overseas or with high age and friends/family overseas can be country-collectors, with the goal to experience something different, without the objective of improving skills or abilities (algorithms 12 and 13, Table 5).

Without high levels of income or education, and without friends and family overseas, but with older age and living in a big city, the motivation to experience something different can be an important element (algorithm 10 in Table 5). If you have older age and living in a big city but you have no higher education and income, and have no friends or family overseas, the combination of experiencing something different with the desire to

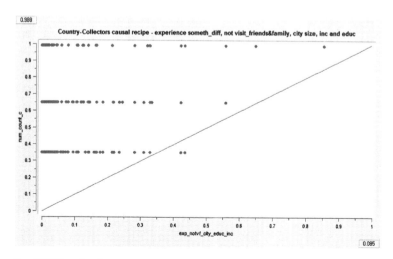

Fig. 5. *XY* Plot for Country-Collectors. Plot of *Y* = Number of Countries Visited by *X* = Combined Causal Condition Configuration (Experience Something Different*Not Visiting Friends and Family*City Size*Education*Income).

Table 5. Fuzzy Set QCA for High Score on Number of Countries Visited.[a]

Algorithm	Model	Raw Coverage	Unique Coverage	Consistency
1	~inc_c*~retired_c*~vis_frds_c*exp_something_d	0.573	0.004	0.736
2	~inc_c*~retired_c*~city_sz_c*exp_something_d	0.490	0.007	0.668
3	~inc_c*~retired_c*exp_something_d*develop_skills_	0.621	0.024	0.778
4	educ_c*~retired_c*city_sz_c*exp_something_d	0.309	0.008	0.833
5	educ_c*~retired_c*exp_something_d*develop_skills_	0.516	0.005	0.817
6	educ_c*~city_sz_c*age_c*~vis_frds_c*exp_something_d	0.221	0.014	0.860
7	~inc_c*~educ_c*~retired_c*~city_sz_c*~age_c*develop_skills_	0.253	0.001	0.894
8	educ_c*~retired_c*~city_sz_c*age_c*~vis_frds_c*~develop_skills_	0.171	0.002	0.924
9	educ_c*~retired_c*~city_sz_c*~age_c*vis_frds_c*~develop_skills_	0.153	0.003	0.936
10	~inc_c*city_sz_c*age_c*~vis_frds_c*exp_something_d*~develop_skills_	0.179	0.008	0.929
11	~inc_c*~educ_c*age_c*~vis_frds_c*exp_something_d*develop_skills_	0.298	0.008	0.916
12	inc_c*educ_c*city_sz_c*~age_c*~vis_frds_c*exp_something_d*~develop_skills_	0.155	0.001	0.978
13	inc_c*educ_c*city_sz_c*age_c*vis_frds_c*exp_something_d*~develop_skills_	0.105	0.001	0.981
14	~inc_c*educ_c*retired_c*city_sz_c*age_c*vis_frds_c*~exp_something_d*~develop_skills_	0.009	0.001	0.810
15	educ_c*~retired_c*~vis_frds_c*exp_something_d	0.486	0.002	0.780
16	educ_c*~retired_c*~age_c*exp_something_d	0.526	0.003	0.777

Notes: Solution coverage: 0.916493; solution consistency: 0.671542; here we have five social-economic status variables (income, age, education, retired, city size) and three reasons to travel (visit friends and family, Experience something different, Develop skills and abilities); sample includes 600 respondents indicating travel overseas in prior 5 years.
[a]Complex solution. Function model: num_count_c = f(inc_c, educ_c, retired_c, city_sz_c, age_c, vis_frds_c, exp_something_d, develop_skills_).

develop skills and abilities is an informative recipe (algorithm 11). For this specific causal recipe, Fig. 6 shows the plot, with most of the cases in or near the upper triangle.

The results show that country-collectors vary in terms of their socioeconomic profiles, and that some reasons to travel can explain how this variation contributes in forming different combinations that explains this heavy-user segment.

"Pull" motives are additional antecedents that may be useful for explaining CC behavior. Pull factors are the attractions that have great appeal for a visitor segment. Among the 15 pull motive items surveyed, six dimensions of activities/sites were identified via exploratory factor analysis: visiting nature and historical sites, visiting nightclubs and casinos, shopping and sightseeing, beaches and theme parks, museums, concerts and musicals, and commercial guided tours.

In mean comparisons, the first dimension (visiting nature and historical sites) had the highest significant difference ($F = 11.413$; $p < 0.001$) among overseas visit segments, and the country-collectors had the highest score in

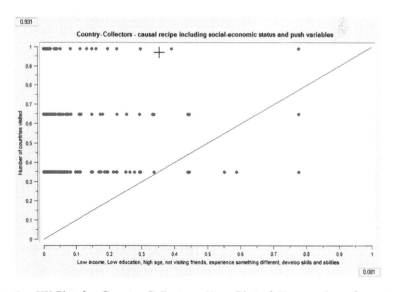

Fig. 6. *XY* Plot for Country-Collectors. *Note:* Plot of Y = number of countries visited by X = combined causal condition configuration (low income*low education*age*not visiting friends/family*experience something different*develop skills and abilities.

114 ARCH G. WOODSIDE ET AL.

a specific question to the sample (the degree of interest about "visiting small towns and countryside," $F = 7.545$; $p = 0.001$).

The socioeconomic variables were combined with the perception of importance of visiting small cities and countryside in order to combine recipes that can result in a high CC membership scores. Table 6 presents the paths resulting from QCA analysis, with two casual recipes including pull antecedents. One recipe includes the combination of high income, high education, big home city, low age, and high perception about visiting small cities and countryside (algorithm 6, Table 6). This specific combination presents high level of consistency (0.967) and a reasonable level of raw coverage (0.201).

The alternative causal recipe includes low income, high age, and high perception of small cities and the countryside in a leisure trip (algorithm 5, Table 6). In this resulting solution, there are recipes, as in algorithm 5, that present lower levels of consistency (0.842) but a high level of raw coverage (0.458, almost 50% of the cases). The plot in Fig. 7 helps to graphically expose the distribution of cases according to the combination of low income and high age, associated with great interest in visiting small towns and the countryside.

The analyses of the CC antecedents are not comprehensive and did not encompass each point explored in the survey in terms of reasons to travel and interest in specific activities. The focus was on the main points, where the country-collectors have high and significant scores. In order to map the antecedents of country-collectors, SES antecedents were analyzed in

Table 6. Fuzzy Set QCA for High Score on Number of Countries Visited.[a]

Algorithm	Model	Raw Coverage	Unique Coverage	Consistency
1	~inc_c*~retired_c	0.745	0.100	0.631
2	educ_c*~retired_c	0.660	0.087	0.704
3	educ_c*~city_sz_c*age_c	0.256	0.005	0.808
4	~inc_c*city_sz_c*age_c	0.242	0.004	0.863
5	~inc_c*age_c*visit_countrysi	0.458	0.012	0.842
6	inc_c*educ_c*city_sz_c*~age_c*visit_countrysi	0.201	0.001	0.967

Notes: Solution coverage: 0.946946; solution consistency: 0.606914; sample includes 600 respondents indicating travel overseas in prior 5 years.
[a]Complex solution. Function model: num_count_c = f(inc_c, educ_c, retired_c, city_sz_c, age_c, visit_countrysi).

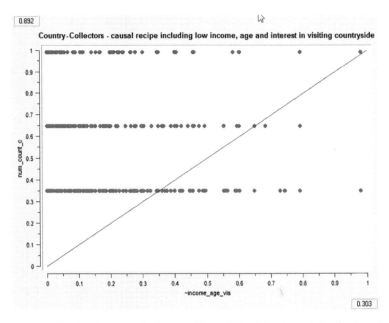

Fig. 7. *XY* Plot for Country-Collectors. Plot of *Y* = Number of Countries Visited by *X* = Combined Causal Condition Configuration (Income*Education*City Size*Low Age_c*Interest in Visiting Countryside).

isolation and these antecedents were then combined with some important "push" motives and the main distinctive attraction in the country-collectors' beliefs.

Characteristics of country-collectors and the Clusters among country-collectors

The number of trips and the number of "collected" countries are not always one and the same. The number of trips abroad can be considered an important part and a causal recipe of being a CC (phi = 1.349; $p < 0.001$). This study shows that over 30% of tourists who have made more than nine trips abroad in the last five years did not visit 6 + countries and, therefore, do not fit this definition of CC. Indeed, some of them visited only one or two countries. The opposite is also true. A small percentage (10%) made few trips and yet fit the definition of CC. A willing traveler with resources can visit half a dozen European countries on a single trip abroad. Thus, although there is a strong association, frequent international travelers are not always country-collectors.

Therefore, country-collectors usually place considerable importance on international leisure trips and remain more than willing to travel again in the near future. Another outcome of being a CC is that they become and/or result in becoming familiar with a substantial number of different countries. Fig. 8 shows a comparison between the degree of familiarity of country-collectors and the other segments with four countries: the United States, Australia, Mainland China, and France.

In each of these four cases, indeed in the case of all seven countries included in the study, country-collectors are more familiar with them. In other words, they are not "novices" within the segment, but are actually experienced travelers who are familiar with the places they visit. The concept of familiarity assumes a broader vision regarding the category of services in question (Park & Lessig, 1981) and this prior knowledge has an influence on the construction of preferences in this category regarding the information that will be "weighed" during decision making and how this information will be used (Coupey, Irwin, & Payne, 1998; Gursoy & McCleary, 2004). Fig. 8 also shows some differences concerning the level of familiarity with the countries under study. The degree of familiarity with the United States surpasses the degree of familiarity with all the other countries (in order to save space, four of the seven countries analyzed were selected). A further observation resulting from Fig. 8 is that geographical proximity does not always mean a higher level of familiarity, even for

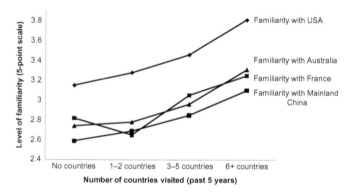

Fig. 8. Familiarity with Specific Countries According to the Number of Countries Visited. *Note*: All the comparisons for the number of countries visited show significant differences with $p < 0.001$ (ANOVA tests).

country-collectors. Although China is geographically closer to Japan, the Japanese respondents are less familiar with mainland China than the other countries under study.

Do country-collectors have a preference to visit countries globally or do they limit themselves to certain geographical regions? With this question in mind, cluster analyses were conducted with a view to identifying, based on the countries visited in the last five years, micro-segments among the country-collectors. Although country-collectors represent a relatively small proportion of consumers of travel and tourism, all members in this segment are unlikely to share the same interest, or the same background, in terms of the countries that collected.

Therefore, a cluster analysis was conducted in an effort to identify clusters according to the countries visited in the past five years. Four groups were identified and the countries visited were mapped by the majority of consumers within each sub-segment. Table 7 summarizes the four clusters,

Table 7. The Clusters inside the Country-Collectors (According to Destinations the Very Most of the Group Visited).

Cluster 1 – East and Pacific (35.1% of CC)	Cluster 2 – Europe and the United States (29.8% of CC)	Cluster 3 – The World (9.6% of CC)	Cluster 4 – East (25.5% of CC)
South Korea	Germany	Germany	Thailand
Mainland China	France	France	Singapore
Hawaii	Italy	Switzerland	Vietnam
Australia	The United Kingdom	Austria	South Korea
Taiwan	The United States	Italy	Mainland China
The United States		The United Kingdom	Taiwan
		Australia	
		New Zealand	
		Thailand	
		Singapore	
		Malaysia	
		Indonesia	
		Vietnam	
		South Korea	
		Mainland China	
		Taiwan	
		Hong Kong	
		The United States	
		Hawaii	
		Guam	

labeled according to the geographical region visited. The first cluster, and the largest, with 35% of the country-collectors, visited Pacific Rim countries, some of which associated with Japan by the Pacific Ocean (Australia and the United States). The second cluster, composed of almost 30% of the country-collectors, mainly visited European countries and the United States.

Most of the members of the third (smallest sub-segment, with almost 10% of the country-collectors) visited almost all the countries under study, and for this reason this cluster was labeled "The World." Finally, the fourth cluster, with 25% of the country-collectors, was basically made up of country-collectors who had visited eastern countries near Japan. Therefore, only a small number of the country-collectors have recently visited several regions of the world. Most have a preference for, or at least have only visited, certain regions and, in the case of the fourth cluster, only neighboring countries.

Dividing into clusters enables additional analyses. In addition to the countries visited, other different traits can be identified among country-collectors. Table 8 shows the mean number of international leisure trips in the last five years. The group, "The World," made approximately 18 trips during this time. The group labeled "East," which traveled to countries close to Japan, made an average number of 12.42 trips during the period in question. The other groups, "East and Pacific" and "Europe and Asia," have made few trips, 9.48 and 8.71, respectively. Segments who travel all over the world and segments whose interest lies in leisure trips to neighboring countries tend to make more international trips for tourism.

Table 9 shows the level of familiarity of the four clusters within the Country-Collectors segment, with seven countries included in the study. Statistical tests show that especially in the case of Italy, France, and the United Kingdom, the group that has recently made trips around the world,

Table 8. Number of Trips Past 5 Years According to the Segment inside Country-Collectors.

Clusters inside CC Segment	Mean	N	Standard Deviation
East and Pacific	9.48	33	3.692
Europe and The United States	8.71	28	4.594
The World	17.89	9	13.486
East	12.42	24	7.552
Total	10.81	94	6.930

ANOVA test ($F = 5.518$; $p = 0.002$); eta^2: 0.155.

Table 9. Familiarity of Country-Collectors Clusters with Specific Countries around the World.

Clusters inside Country-Collectors (According with Destinations)		Familiarity with United States	Familiarity with Italy	Familiarity with France	Familiarity with Australia	Familiarity with The United Kingdom	Familiarity with Mainland China	Familiarity with South Korea
East and Pacific	Mean	3.82	2.39	2.58	3.24	2.58	3.09	3.70
	N	33	33	33	33	33	33	33
	Standard deviation	0.77	1.00	0.97	0.94	1.17	1.04	0.95
Europe and The United States	Mean	3.96	3.96	4.04	3.50	4.07	2.89	3.32
	N	28	28	28	28	28	28	28
	Standard deviation	0.79	0.84	0.74	1.17	1.12	1.40	1.16
The World	Mean	4.22	4.11	3.89	3.56	4.11	3.67	3.67
	N	9	9	9	9	9	9	9
	Standard deviation	0.67	0.60	0.60	1.33	0.60	0.71	1.22
East	Mean	3.50	3.50	3.04	3.13	2.71	3.17	3.46
	N	24	24	24	24	24	24	24
	Standard deviation	0.78	0.78	0.95	0.90	1.08	0.92	1.06
Total	Mean	3.82	3.31	3.26	3.32	3.20	3.11	3.52
	N	94	94	94	94	94	94	94
	Standard deviation	0.79	1.11	1.07	1.04	1.29	1.11	1.06

Notes: The significant differences were with Italy ($F = 20.517$; $p < 0.001$; eta$^2 = 0.406$), France ($F = 16, 117$; $p < 0.001$; eta$^2 = 0.349$) and the United Kingdom ($F = 13.194$; $p < 0.001$; eta$^2 = 0.305$). Based on a 5-point scale from 1 (not familiar at all) to 5 (extremely familiar).

followed by the group that has mainly visited Europe and the United States, high means of familiarity. Furthermore, even the groups that have not recently visited the United States, such as the "East" group, have a reasonable level of familiarity with the country and similar to or greater than that of neighboring countries such as South Korea and Mainland China.

Another statistical comparison that provided insight into the clusters within the Country Collector segment had to do with the motives for traveling, the dimensions of which have already been mentioned in this text. One of the dimensions in which significant differences can be seen is the need to "increase social visibility." In this specific dimension, "The World" sub-segment has a higher mean than the rest. In this case, the fact that they wish to build a collection of stories to tell about the countries they have visited and that this adds to their prestige among the people around them is an important factor. A study by Andersen et al. (2000) on Japanese visitors to Scotland mentions a cluster identified as "Collectors," who seek prestige while collecting their consumer experiences. See Table 10 for further details.

Another dimension with significant differences is based on the need to "learn skills and knowledge." In this case, the "Europe and USA" and "The World" CC sub-segments have higher means than the others. The fact that Europe and the United States are viewed as traditional centers of culture and learning possibly leads to them being effective choices when the aim of the trip is not only sightseeing and tourisms but to learn something new for professional or personal use. Studies such as that of Cha et al. (1995) and Jang et al. (2002), based on overseas Japanese travelers, also cite knowledge as a key motive and includes cluster labeled "novelty."

No significant differences appear among the CC sub-segments regarding socioeconomic-geographical status (age, gender, household income, education, employment status, marital status, and home city in Japan).

The Outcomes of Being a Country Collector and the Perceptions and Intentions of the United States

Seven specific countries in different geographical regions were examined in-depth in the study: the United States, Italy, France, Australia, the United Kingdom, Mainland China, and South Korea. The intention was to ask the respondent to say which country was the best example of certain attributes, irrespective of whether or not the respondent had already visited that country. In addition to comparing the countries with one another, in

Table 10. The Clusters inside Country-Collectors and the Means Comparison Relates to Each "Push" Motive Dimension.

Clusters inside Country-Collectors		Searching New Experiences	Increase Social Visibility	Searching for Peace/Relaxing	Learning Skills/ Knowledge	Visit Friends and Family	Be with Others Who Enjoy Same Thing as I do
East and Pacific	Mean	4.58	2.83	4.06	3.42	2.82	3.82
	N	33	33	33	33	33	33
	Standard deviation	0.44	0.94	0.73	0.94	1.29	1.16
Europe and The United States	Mean	4.62	3.11	4.36	4.25	3.11	3.89
	N	28	28	28	28	28	28
	Standard deviation	0.44	0.93	0.62	0.81	1.47	1.03
The World	Mean	4.50	3.92	4.00	4.17	3.22	3.67
	N	9	9	9	9	9	9
	Standard deviation	0.40	0.65	0.66	0.71	1.20	1.12
East	Mean	4.38	2.71	3.92	3.60	2.96	3.50
	N	24	24	24	24	24	24
	Standard deviation	0.51	0.79	0.76	0.81	1.30	0.88
Total	Mean	4.53	2.98	4.11	3.79	2.98	3.74
	N	94	94	94	94	94	94
	Standard deviation	0.46	0.93	0.71	0.91	1.33	1.05

Notes: Using ANOVA tests, significant differences were found in dimension "Increase social visibility" ($F = 4.702$; $p = 0.004$; $eta^2 = 0.135$) and dimension. "Learning skills/knowledge" ($F = 5.717$; $p = 0.001$; $eta^2 = 0.160$); the items inside each dimension were measured with a 5-point scale, from 1 strongly disagree to 5 strongly agree.

the opinion of the country-collectors and others who took part in the study, these questions enable a comparison between the perception of those who had not visited the United States during the past five years and those who actually had.

Therefore, the independent variable under study was the number of countries visited in the past five years and the outcome variable was the perception (share of each country) in relation to the attribute. As Woodside and Dubelaar (2002) discuss, potential visitors' evaluations are likely to show expectations concerning how much visitors will enjoy their experiences in their destination region, but this preliminary evaluation is subjected to substantial revision after the place has actually been visited.

Four exhibits (Figs. 9–12) show the results of four attributes that vary from one country to another. In order to save space, only the three countries with best represent each attribute – with the highest indices – have been selected, and for each country there are two lines, comparing respondents among those who have visited the United States and those who have not. This additional division in this analysis is in order to visualize the possible differences.

The first attribute to be analyzed was "friendly people and hospitality." Fig. 9 shows the results for Australia, South Korea, and the United States for the countries with the best ranking for this attribute among the seven countries in the survey. Among people who have not visited the United States in the past five years, in every segment except that of country-collectors, who visited six or more countries, Australia is the country that appears most frequently. The United States is not viewed as "friendly" by non-visitors. The situation changes among those who did visit the United States. In this case, the United States has higher indices than South Korea and is equal to Australia in the eyes of country-collectors.

Fig. 10 shows the share of respondents in each segment concerning the attribute "variety of things to do and places to see." Here, the United States has a higher share than France and Australia, and there are also differing opinions among those who had not visit the United States and those who visited it for leisure in the last five years. Among those who visited the United States recently, the CC segments had a lower share than the two previous segments (those who traveled to one or two countries and those who visited between three and five countries).

Despite the perception of variety of places to see and things to do when visiting the United States, the country does not fare so well when the subject is beautiful scenery. When it comes to tourists that had not visited the United States recently, there is quite a marked difference between Australia

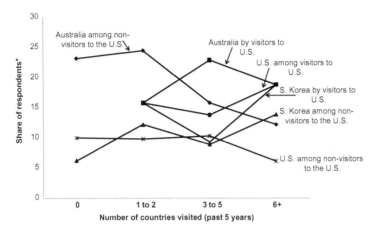

Fig. 9. Share of Respondents of the Most Appropriate Country According to Item "Friendly People and Hospitality." *Note*: Respondents had seven countries to select one from in responding to the question, "Which country offers the best representation of this attribute": The United States, Italy, France, Australia, the United Kingdom, Mainland China, and South Korea.

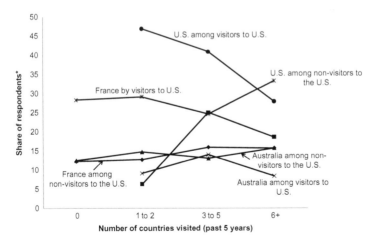

Fig. 10. Share of Respondents of the Most Appropriate Country According to Item "Variety of Thing to do and Places to See." *Note*: Respondents had seven countries to select one from in responding to the question "Which country offers the best representation of this attribute": The United States, Italy, France, Australia, the United Kingdom, Mainland China, and South Korea.

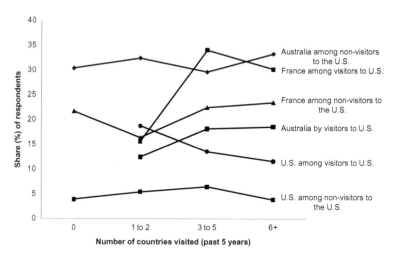

Fig. 11. Share of Respondents of the Most Appropriate Country According to Item "Beautiful Scenery." *Note*: Respondents had seven countries to select one from in responding to the question "Which country offers the best representation of this attribute": The United States, Italy, France, Australia, the United Kingdom, Mainland China, and South Korea.

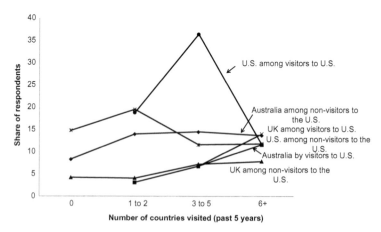

Fig. 12. Share of Respondents of the Most Appropriate Country According to Item "Good Customer Service." *Note*: Respondents had seven countries to select one from in responding to the question "Which country offers the best representation of this attribute": The United States, Italy, France, Australia, the United Kingdom, Mainland China, and South Korea.

and the United States in all segments (for both non-travelers and recent visitors). For recent visitors to the United States, there is a significant drop in this difference. An interesting contrast occurs in the segment of those who visited one or two countries in the past five years where one of them is the United States. For these travelers, the share of the United States is slightly higher than that of France and Australia. In this case, presence in a specific country (the United States) was separated and analyzed; these analyses informs the conclusion that the difference in perception in relation to the different countries can change considerably after these countries have been visited, possibly altering the consumer decision. Consumers who experience a particular country tend to alter their perception, and in the case of the United States for the better. See Fig. 11 for additional details.

Findings for a final attribute appear in Fig. 12, "good customer service." The United States generally fares better than the United Kingdom and Australia, and in this specific case, analyzing visitors and non-visitors to the United States, a difference in the share occurs only in the segment of travelers who had recently visited three to five countries for the purpose of leisure. In this segment, among those who had visited the United States, the United States predominates as a synonym of good customer service. A difference occurs between who actually experienced the United States and those who built their perception based on other sources or on a visit further into the past.

Along the same lines, but analyzing specifically the general Japanese impression of the United States, on a ten-point scale, one can see from Fig. 13 the difference, whether they are Country-Collectors or not, between those who had paid a recent visit to United States and those who had not.

Another question sought to discover whether and how the general impression of respondents regarding the United States has changed over the past five years. The results appear in Table 11. The more countries they have visited, the larger the share of people who changed their opinion of the country for the better. In the case of the country-collectors, a smaller portion mentioned that their impression did not change at all during this time. Some report changes for the worse (18.1%) and others for the better (24.5%). The country-collectors, having built up more experiences and visited more countries, seem more sensitive to reevaluations over time.

As for the future behavior of the country-collectors, some insights do appear. Analyzing the participants' future choice to visit the United States, when it comes to organizing the trip, there is a considerable difference between those who opt for a package tour and those who opt for independent travel. Fig. 14 shows these differences. According to these results, the

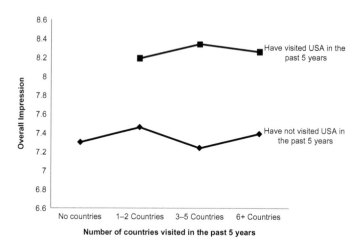

Fig. 13. Overall Impression about the United States between People Who Have Visited United States in the Past 5 Years and People Who Have Not.

Table 11.   Differences in Overall in the Last Five Years.

			Change of Overall Impression about The United States			
			Gets worse than 5 years ago	Has not changed	Gets better than 5 years ago	Total
Numbers of countries visited past 5 years	No countries	Count	51	488	61	600
		%	8.5%	81.3%	10.2%	100.0%
	One to two countries	Count	21	257	46	324
		%	6.5%	79.3%	14.2%	100.0%
	Three to five countries	Count	15	137	30	182
		%	8.2%	75.3%	16.5%	100.0%
	Six or more countries	Count	17	54	23	94
		%	18.1%	57.4%	24.5%	100.0%
Total		Count	104	936	160	1,200
		%	8.7%	78.0%	13.3%	100.0%

Note: Significant differences (phi = 0.164; $p < 0.001$).

more countries that a person visits, the more she/he tends to opt for independent travel, with the highest rate of independent travel preference occurring among country-collectors and if the traveler has already visited the country in question this difference grows even more. Familiarity with the

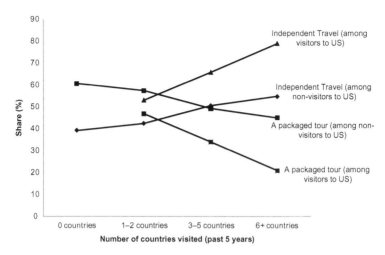

Fig. 14. The Type of Travel Chosen, If Traveling to United States for Leisure Purpose.

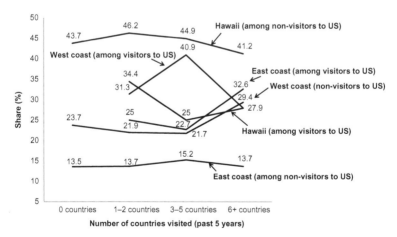

Fig. 15. When Thinking about Traveling to the United States, the Part of the Country that Comes to Mind. *Notes*: Respondents had six options to select one from in responding to the question. "When thinking of traveling to the United States for leisure purpose, which part of the country comes to mind first?" The other three options presented (Guam, other parts of the United States, and the whole country including the US mainland and islands) received less than 10% each.

country and the experience of country-collectors with international tourism may account for this preference to travel independently.

The fact that a traveler has visited the country also alters how he perceives the different regions of the United States. Fig. 15 shows the results concerning what comes to mind when the respondent is asked about a trip to the United States. Among those who have not visited the United States, most think of Hawaii, followed by the west coast and then the east coast.

The country-collectors tend to think more of the west coast than the other groups. Among those who have visited the United States in the past five years, the first place that comes to mind is Hawaii (among those who have visited one or two countries) or the west coast (among those who have visited between three and five countries). But among the country-collectors, the east coast comes first (33%), above the other two regions which might be considered more famous in terms of tourism (both with 28%). How country-collectors remember and see the United States is different from travelers and non-travelers in the other segments.

CONCLUSIONS, LIMITATIONS, AND IMPLICATIONS

The present study analyzes the results of a three-city survey conducted in Japan to explore a conceptually new segment in the field of tourism: country-collectors. The study provides profiles of the antecedents of this segment and how it is composed and explores the intentions, perceptions, and attitudes of this segment.

Robert Stebbins (2009, p. 46) claims, "The world of tourism is rich in opportunities for conspicuous consumption and the creation of identities that flow from a person's travels." He describes the concept, "serious leisure," which means the systematic pursuit of an amateur, hobbyist, or volunteer activity that participants find so substantial and interesting that they launch themselves on a career centering on acquiring and expressing its special skills, knowledge, and experience (Stebbins, 2004a, 2004b). The analysis presented in this study demonstrates that the CC segment is highly involved with international travel; such travel is a priority in their lives. Belk, Wallendorf, and Sherry (1989) discusses the distinction between sacred and profane travel, and that a part of any touring involves seeking the sacred. Sacred, as Solomon (2013) describes, does not necessarily carry a religious meaning, but involves objects and events from normal activities which are treated with respect or awe.

Contemporary consumers may regard some experiences as sacred (Belk et al., 1989). According to Stebbins (2004a, 2004b), to understand the meaning of such leisure is significant when it comes to understanding their motivation for the pursuit. Driven by the need to experience something different and/or develop abilities and knowledge, or counting on some facilities, such as having relatives and friends overseas, appears to motivate country-collectors to start collecting countries. As country-collectors indulge in this leisure with a high degree of underlying seriousness, they develop a high degree of familiarity, perceptions, and attitudes/intentions that differ from other leisure travelers.

From a marketing perspective, country-collectors only according to their social and economic profiles is impossible. To describe better who they are, recipes (combinations of personal and situational characteristics and reasons for going on a leisure trip) should be taken into account; such recipes will likely help in the design of effective tourism services and communication messages. Some combinations of demographic and economic variables and reasons for leisure travel are found in recipes that account for the origin of a CC member. The QCA method is exceptional for analyzing complex causation.

Evaluating the clusters identified within the CC segment, based on the patterns and backgrounds of destinations experienced, satisfies the need to target segments. Such actions should seek not only to identify country-collectors (this heavy-user target of international travels) but also to explore the micro-segments among heavy users. Using relationship marketing tools, narrowing down contact with micro-segments may be highly effective.

The study shows that the perception, interests, and intentions of country-collectors differ from those of other segments of travelers and non-travelers. Despite Kenseth's (1991) findings regarding the collection of experiences (he finds that repeating an experience may not serve the desires of collectors), the present study shows that country-collectors are far more interested in visiting the same countries again than other groups of travelers and non-travelers. This orientation to repeat visits to countries should not be taken to imply that country-collectors have less interest in visiting additional countries for the first time. Simply, the CC segment places great importance on past behavior in planning future leisure trips.

The fact that the study is fundamentally based on one survey conducted in a specific country and the data are based on closed questions suggests a need for studies to probe further into how country-collectors think, and decide, and act. The findings here are explorable in-depth with the use of case study methods designed for such a purpose. This theme would also serve as a suitable extension of studies involving the collection of experiences which, according to prior studies, do not focus necessarily on tourism (Keinan & Kivetz, 2011; Ratner et al., 1999).

REFERENCES

Andersen, V., Prentice, R., & Watanabe, K. (2000). Journey for experiences: Japanese independent travelers in Scotland. *Journal of Travel and Tourism Marketing, 9*(1/2), 129–151.
Belk, R. W. (1982). Acquiring, possessing, and collecting: Fundamental processes in consumer behavior. In R. F. Bushard & S. D. Hunt (Eds.), *Marketing theory: Philosophy of science perspectives* (pp. 185–190). Chicago, IL: American Marketing Association.
Belk, R. W. (1988). Possessions and the extended self. *Journal of Consumer Research, 15*(September), 139–168.
Belk, R. W. (1991). The ineluctable mysteries of possessions. *Journal of Social Behavior and Personality, 6*(6), 17–55.
Belk, R. W. (1995). *Collecting in a consumer society.* London: Routledge.
Belk, R. W., Wallendorf, M., & Sherry, J. F., Jr. (1989). The sacred and the profane in consumer behavior: Theodicy on the Odyssey. *Journal of Consumer Research, 16*(1), 1–38.
Belk, R. W., Wallendorf, M., Sherry, J. F., Jr., Holbrook, M., & Roberts, S. (1988). Collectors and collecting. In M. Houston (Ed.), *Advances in consumer research* (Vol. 15). Provo, UT: Association for Consumer Research.
Carey, C. (2008). Modeling collecting behavior: The role of set completion. *Journal of Economic Psychology, 29*, 336–347.
Case, D. O. (2009). Serial collecting as leisure, and coin collecting in particular. *Library Trends, 57*(4), 729–752.
Cha, S., McCleary, K., & Uysal, M. (1995). Travel motivations of Japanese overseas travelers: A factor-cluster segmentation approach. *Journal of Travel Research, 34*(1), 33–39.
Coupey, E., Irwin, J. R., & Payne, J. W. (1998). Product familiarity and preference construction. *Journal of Consumer Research, 24*(4), 459–468.
Feller, R. (2011). *Collecting away their suffering: Meaningful hobbies and the processing of traumatic experience.* Keene, New Hampshire: Antioch University New England.
Gursoy, D., & McCleary, K. W. (2004). An integrative model of tourists' information search behavior. *Annals of Tourism Research, 31*(2), 353–373.
Jang, S. C., Morrison, A. M., & O'Leary, J. T. (2002). Benefit segmentation of Japanese pleasure travelers to the USA and Canada: Selecting target markets based on the profitability and risk of individual market segments. *Tourism Management, 23*, 367–378.
Keinan, A., & Kivetz, R. (2011). Productivity orientation and the consumption of collectable experiences. *Journal of Consumer Research, 7*(6), 935–950.
Kenseth, J. (1991). *The age of the marvelous.* Hanover, NH: Hood Museum of Art.
King, L. M., & Prideaux, B. (2010). Special interest tourists collecting places and destinations: A case study of Australian world heritage sites. *Journal of Vacation Marketing, 16*, 235–247.
Kotler, P., & Keller, K. L. (2009). *Marketing management.* Englewood Cliffs, NJ: Pearson Prentice Hall.

Lee, T. H., & Crompton, J. (1992). Measuring novelty seeking in tourism. *Annals of Tourism Research, 19*(4), 732–751.

McIntosh, W. D., & Schmeichel, B. (2004). Collectors and collecting: A social psychological perspective. *Leisure Sciences, 26*(1), 85–97.

Park, W., & Lessig, V. P. (1981). Familiarity and its impact on consumer decision biases and heuristics. *Journal of Consumer Research, 8*(2), 223–231.

Petrick, J. (2002). An examination of golf vacationers' novelty. *Annals of Tourism Research, 29*(2), 384–400.

Pine, B. J., & Gilmore, J. H. (1998). Welcome to the experience economy. *Harvard Business Review, (July–August), 76*, 97–105.

Pine, B. J., & Gilmore, J. H. (1999). *The experience economy*. Boston, MA: Harvard Business School Press.

Ragin, C. C. (2008). *Redesigning social inquiry: Fuzzy sets and beyond*. Chicago, IL: University of Chicago Press.

Ratner, R. K., Kahn, B. E., & Kahneman, D. (1999). Choosing less-preferred experiences for the sake of variety. *Journal of Consumer Research, 26*, 1–15.

Saari, L. (1997). Those crazy collectors. *The Orange County Register*, April 15, p. D1.

Schultz, P. (2010). *1,000 Places to see before you die* (Updated ed.). New York, NY: Workman.

Snepenger, D. J. (1987). Segmenting the vacation market by novelty-seeking role. *Journal of Travel Research, 26*(2), 8–14.

Solomon, M. R. (2013). *Consumer behavior: Buying, having, and being*. Upper Saddle River, NJ: Pearson.

Stebbins, R. A. (2004a). Erasing the line between work and leisure in North America. Paper presented at the "Leisure and Liberty in North America" conference. Retrieved from http://people.ucalgary.ca/~stebbins/leisurelibertyinnpap.pdf. Accessed on June 7, 2012.

Stebbins, R. A. (2004b). *Between work & leisure*. New Brunswick: Transaction Publishers.

Stebbins, R. A. (2009). *Leisure and consumption: Common ground/ separate worlds*. New York, NY: Palgrave Macmillan.

Timothy, D. J. (1998). Collecting places: Geodetic lines in tourist space. *Journal of Travel & Tourism Marketing, 7*(4), 123–129.

Tung, V. W. S., & Ritchie, J. R. B. (2011). Exploring the essence of memorable tourism experiences. *Annals of Tourism Research, 38*(4), 1367–1386.

Twedt, D. W. (1964). How important to marketing strategy is the "Heavy User"? *Journal of Marketing, 28*(January), 71–72.

Waterlow, L. (2012). *There goes the bride … women say they would rather travel the world than get married*. Retrieved from http://www.dailymail.co.uk/femail/article-2139482/There-goes-bride-Women-say-travel-world-married.html. Accessed on May 4, 2012.

Woodside, A. G., Cook, V. J., & Mindak, W. (1987). Profiling the heavy traveler segment. *Journal of Travel Research, 25*, 9–14.

Woodside, A. G., & Dubelaar, C. (2002). A general theory of tourism consumption systems: A conceptual framework and an empirical exploration. *Journal of Travel Research, 41*, 120–132.

Woodside, A. G., Hsu, S.-Y., & Marshall, R. (2011). General theory of culture's consequences on international tourism behavior. *Journal of Business Research, 64*, 785–799.

Woodside, A. G., & Zhang, M. (2012). Identifying x-consumers using casual recipes: "Whales" and "Jumbo Shrimps" casino gamblers. *Journal of Gambling Studies, 28*, 13–26.

APPENDIX

Unlike statistical tests based on matrix algebra (which tests for symmetrical relationships between independent variables and a dependent variable), QCA tests are based on Boolean algebra and test asymmetric relationships. A Pearson product-moment correlation test for the degree of fit of data to a symmetric relationship, that is, high values of the independent variable associate with high values of the dependent variables and low values of the independent variable associate with low values of the dependent variable. Statistical tests of a relationship take the stance that a relationship between an independent variable and a dependent variable is large when the relationship is both necessary and sufficient (i.e., symmetrical). QCA test whether or not a sufficiency only relationship occurs between an antecedent condition (analogous to "independent variable") and an outcome condition (analogous to "dependent variable").

High sufficiency occurs when high values of the antecedent condition associate with high values of the outcome condition – QCA makes no prediction about low values of the antecedent condition and the values of the outcome condition.

High sufficiency but not necessary conditions are the type of relationships that occur frequently in real-life – most important relationships between two unique variables ("conditions" in the parlance of QCA) show high sufficiency but are not necessary for a high value to occur in an outcome condition because other antecedent conditions exit that associate with high outcome values. Fig. A1 shows four types of relationships: (a) rectangular ($r \approx 0.0$); (b) symmetrical ($r \approx 1.0$); (c) asymmetrical showing sufficiency ($r \approx 0.40$); (d) asymmetrical showing necessity ($r \approx 0.40$) for 20 different cases of data.

QCA most frequently finds that a few (i.e., 4–10) complex antecedent conditions among 80 or more possible complex conditions are useful in that they indicate high sufficiency in predicting high scores for the outcome condition without any one of the complex antecedent conditions predicting being necessary for a high score to occur in the outcome condition. A "complex antecedent condition" is the conjoining of two or more simple antecedent conditions and it represents the logical "and" condition. The lowest score among the conjoined scores of two or more simple antecedent conditions represents the logical "and condition."

All conditions, all simple antecedent and outcome conditions are calibrated before testing for sufficiency in fsQCA. In calibrating scores, the

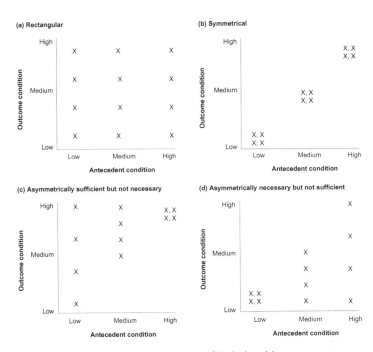

Fig. A1. Four Types of Relationships.

original scores are converted to scores ranging from 0.00 to 1.00 with the calibrated scores representing the degree of membership in the condition. See Ragin (2008) for additional details on calibration testing for sufficiency.